KARL RAHNER

His Life, Thought and Works

KARL RAHNER

His Life, Thought and Works

by
HERBERT VORGRIMLER

Translated by
EDWARD QUINN

DEUS BOOKS
PAULIST PRESS
(Paulist Fathers)
Glen Rock, N. J.

A Deus Books Edition of Paulist Press, 1966, by special arrangement with Burns & Oates Ltd., London, S.W.1.

This is a translation of Karl Rahner—Leben, Denken, Werke (*Manz Verlag, Munich*) *originally published by Uitgeverij Lannoo in Tielt under the title* Karl Rahner—Denkers over God en Wereld.

Nihil obstat: Carolus McGowan, B.A.

  Censor deputatus

Imprimatur: Patritius Casey

  Vicarius Generalis

Westmonasterii: die 23a Octobris 1965

Published by Paulist Press
Editorial Office: 304 W. 58 St., N.Y. 19, N.Y.
Business Office: Glen Rock, N.J.

Printed and bound in the United States
of America by Our Sunday Visitor Press

Contents

1 Karl Rahner's Life

In a brief introduction to the life, thought and work of a theologian, a priest and a religious, is it wholly right to begin by naming his birth-place and giving the exact setting of his native-land? For the *theologian*, in the second millennium of the history of the Church of Christ, it is no longer possible to begin to practise theology relying entirely and solely on himself. His spiritual and therefore his first home is the meditation of the Church of all ages on the inexhaustible Word of God. He has to be at home with God's people in the Old Testament, in its covenant-theology, its expectation of ultimate and final salvation in the Messiah, its afflictions from without and its divisions within: the people in which God's Word became flesh. He has to be able to follow the magnificent development of patristic thought in which the last phase of ancient philosophy—neoplatonism—confronted divine revelation and found there its supreme and unexpected confirmation: that finite man comes to share in the divine being itself and returns to his origin in a gradual process of divinization. He will always be indebted to the clear, systematic thought of scholasticism with its firm statement of principles, particularly to St Thomas Aquinas, in whom theological reflection perhaps took the first great step forward from ancient, cosmocentric to modern, personalist philosophy. The theologian finally has to understand his own time, the thinking, hoping, dreaming of men of every "today", to whom he has to relate and expound the Gospel, but who also from their standpoint can assist him to a deeper understanding of the Word of God. And is not the *priest* also, as it were, without an earthly home and ancestors? At least he ought to be so. The priest belongs to the order of Melchisedech, the priest-king of whom it is said in Scripture: "No name of father or mother, no pedigree, no date of birth or of death; there he stands, eternally, a priest, the true figure of the Son of God" (Heb. 7.3). Greater than that of his first home, given him by nature, is the family which the priest calls his own: "If anyone does the will of my Father who is in heaven, he is my brother, and sister, and mother" (Matt. 12.50). That applies most of all to the *religious*.

Here we are concerned with the life of a Jesuit. This involves a paradox: for being a Jesuit means to push private affairs into the background and to regard them as secondary. First and last in the Society of Jesus come service, discipline, obedience, selflessness: not for the sake of the smooth functioning of the institution, but because this is the only way in which man can really bear witness to the infinite grandeur and mystery of God. This absolute service which a man accepts in becoming a Jesuit not only forbids any cult of the person and any parade of himself as a star, but requires him also on entering the order, and at any future time when it seems necessary, to break off all contact with the past. In the foundation of Ignatius of Loyola the Spanish and German conceptions of military service were more or less naturally fused into a remarkable synthesis, a synthesis which of its nature cannot appeal to everyone. Once a person has experienced and obeyed this vocation the description of that man is, strictly speaking, already complete.

These general remarks will explain what is essential in the person of Karl Rahner. He is unreservedly a Jesuit. Why he became one, is not for us to say: it must be accepted as a fact. The essential characteristics of the Society of Jesus are so imprinted upon him that they have become the essential characteristics of his personality. He is first of all wholly and unstintingly the Church's man, a servant of the Catholic Church: her affairs, concerns and problems have become his own most intimate affairs, concerns and problems. It is his aim to serve the Church in that absolute form which is proper to the Society of Jesus: in obedience to his superiors. This means working precisely where one is needed at any particular moment and, once there, in allowing oneself to be used. Undoubtedly such a way of life in our modern society seems, when closely examined, shocking and revolting. Undoubtedly also it provides innumerable opportunities for cheap and silly comment (such as "corpse-like obedience"). No one has explained more finely than Hans Urs von Balthasar how little this implies the annihilation of humanity: "In the last resort, you alone are, and are all in all. And we are not, for what is good in us is already you; and what we are ourselves is not worth considering. In your presence we diminish and want to be nothing but your mirror and a window for our brethren. Our decline before you is your ascendancy over us, our consummation in you and your entry into us." Such a life is scarcely credible in this age and particularly in our world. But it continues to be lived by some.

That had to be said from the beginning, for the reader must not expect to find here details of Karl Rahner's private life. In fact, there would be little enough to relate. He is a theologian, at the service of his order; he has no private property and cannot dispose of his income; he lives in a Jesuit house, in a room furnished with the utmost simplicity and which—like other members of his order—he himself keeps clean and tidy. We can say that he works unceasingly at theology, so that a list of his books and articles already numbers nearly a thousand; that he has chosen to interest the public in these things and has travelled all over Europe, speaking in halls filled to overflowing; that he has addressed cardinals and bishops at the Council; or that his writings have been translated into more than ten languages. What more can be said of his "private life"? He rises after a few hours' sleep, says Mass, makes his prescribed meditation, reads his office, answers letters or applies himself to study, so that he already has a whole day's work behind him when others are just beginning. Only after this come the lectures, visits, and finally writing articles and books until late into the night.

There is simply no place here for the more light-hearted interests. It cannot be said of him, for instance, as it is said of some other theologians, that they are connoisseurs of wine, botanical experts, keen mountaineers or skiers. Yet it would be false to conclude from the absence of these brighter spots that his existence is joyless and heartless. Hundreds of Karl Rahner's listeners can relate how often otherwise dry occasions were studded with examples of his humour, how he enjoys a joke and how gladly he seizes on a forceful expression.

We can—indeed, we must—mention another aspect of his "private" life. There are many poor people in different places who have been helped by him. He possesses nothing himself, but when he hears of a person's need he is able to tap the sources of material aid; I am inclined to think also that he sizes up the people to whom he appeals by their readiness to help. Pastoral care and spiritual aid in the form of letters and interviews lasting for hours also deserve to be mentioned at least briefly here. I have often observed how gladly he finds time for a troubled soul who stops him on the street—at least as willingly as for theologians who come from a distance to consult him.

Here, I think, lie the roots of Karl Rahner's "existential" theology: he is quite literally a "sympathetic" person. "Existential" does not mean only—as I shall explain in the second part of this book—remaining in contact with the thought of the present time. It means first of all that, in his professional work as a theologian and in his "private" life, he is always wholly concerned with the religious basis of the human situation. Seen from this standpoint, his theology may be described as "kerygmatic theology"; but the term is liable to be misunderstood. For Rahner it does not mean that alongside the necessarily abstract and dry, strictly scientific theology, there must be a diluted form "for wider circles"; nor does it mean that he is opposed to subtle, highly specialized theological studies. It is simply a difference of horizon.

He wants to liberate theological formulas and concepts from the rigidity they have acquired as mere tools, without throwing them aside and without questioning their value and importance in the Church's theological tradition—as the modernists of all ages do. Out of consideration for the reader, for man's sake, he restores to the concepts and formulas of text-book theology their dignity as embodiments of the living word, not brandishing them or juggling with them, but seeking out the reality in them (not elsewhere) and then seizing on the reality itself. Because he has first experienced man as a questioner, he has mastered the art of questioning and questions himself ruthlessly. He is opposed to all merely habitual ways of thinking, to intellectual sloth, to self-satisfaction, whose practitioners always know without further thought all that a word implies. Such lifeless apathy will always lack that which is offered in abundance in Karl Rahner's theology and which distinguishes

11

all the great philosophers: wonder at the reality itself which reveals itself to the questioner and—taking him by surprise—enlightens him.

In addition to all this, he possesses the unusual gift of stating what he has thought out. Rahner rightly counts as one of the few contemporary thinkers who has acquired an unmistakable style. It is not a style that is easily accessible: it creates work for hearer and reader. But a guide to Karl Rahner's work must certainly explore the peculiarities of his style. We might say that this consists of two components and an "alienating effect", which secures their sequence and co-ordination.

The first component is an attempt, with the aid of all the possibilities of language—above all of the participles, otherwise little used in German—so to express the known truth that the formal repetition of concepts finally reveals the reality itself, without the concepts being thereby devalued: in other words in such a sentence there resounds—so to speak—all the past achievement of theology, wrapped up in secondary conditional clauses and in innumerable participles. Incidentally, no expert can fail to observe that this resonance presupposes immense historical and systematic knowledge: in a word, sheer industry. Rahner's definition of grace and nature provide a good example of this first component of his style:

> Grace is the *a priori* capacity for the connatural reception of God's self-disclosure in word (faith-charity) and in the beatific vision. Nature is man's permanent state presupposed in his being able to listen, in such a form that the sinner and unbeliever can close his mind to this persistent self-disclosure of God without (as in a culpable denial of his metaphysical essence) at the same time implicitly affirm-

ing what is denied; in such a form also that this self-disclosure can appear to man once created as an absolutely free miracle of personal love, which he cannot demand "of himself" (by nature), although it can be addressed to him and he is essentially open to it (nature as a positive *potentia obedientialis* for supernatural grace).[1]

The theologian will find in this lengthy statement a complete summary of doctrine on grace; he will find correctly stated the Church's teaching on the relationship between nature and grace; and yet in Rahner's language the thing itself becomes clearer than before and in his formulation touches the hearer more directly ("God's self-disclosure", "free miracle of personal love"). The statement of course is not simple and a person who cannot understand it at first reading need not think that he is stupid. Nor was the sentence produced in a day, nor even in a year. It has to be read twice, three times, and every word must be kept in mind throughout the process. This naturally presupposes good will and some effort. Theology advances only by retaining what has been previously established and then questioning this anew and more deeply; but many Christians and not a few theologians hesitate to make the effort of constant questioning: they expect rather to perceive in a theological or religious work what they have already known for a long time, and to find those categories within which their thought is accustomed to proceed. But the Word of God, for ever inexhaustible, did not go out into the world merely to confirm theology and the time and energies of a theologian are too precious to be consumed in sterile repetition of the same thing. Karl Rahner's style eludes lazy minds. The genuine listener is fascinated by the perfectly apt, complex statement, because it is almost

13

overflowing with data and queries (the first component of Rahner's style).

A reader is also directly involved in the *second component*, which I would describe as the element of religious pathos and which in most of Rahner's works is found interspersed in the midst of rigorously scientific statements. This sudden turn of style is what I called the "alienating effect". Thus we read in a technical theological essay on the hypostatic union:

> God's remoteness is the incomprehensibility of his all-penetrating proximity: this is the message of Christmas. He is tenderly present. He is near. He touches the heart gently with his love. He says: "Do not fear." In prison he is at hand. If, when we begin to seek him, we think that he is not present it is because there was never a moment in our life when we did not possess him in the unobtrusive sweetness of his ineffable love. He is present like pure light, concealed because everywhere diffused, as, in the silent humility of its nature, his light making everything else visible. Christmas tells you in your solitude: Trust your surroundings, they are not emptiness; let go and you will find; renounce and you will be rich.[2]

Sentences like these, full of religious pathos, are not introduced into Rahner's work as rhetorical tricks; and it would be offensive to speak of "sentimentality". The point is that the original pastoral aspect of his theology becomes visible here: it is his intention, not to provide theoretical instruction alone, but also to assist man to experience grace. In a world where technology and industry loom so large that it seems impossible for man to realize anything unless it is produced and controlled by hand, Rahner's message is for many a decisive aid to an experience of their own transcendence and therein to an experience of God.

Here, too, we can see a fundamental "weakness" of Rahner's. Because he knows man's deep religious need and because this is of considerable concern to him, he thinks that every other theologian in the Church must feel the same. And when he finds that their feelings are in no way involved, he cannot easily conceal his disappointment. That is the reason—and that alone—for his occasional harsh comments on the theology of the schools which does not manage to go beyond the mere repetition of the same concepts (rigidly applied and perhaps never properly understood) or to see through them the truths they would express, thus failing to explain them in the form of healing responses to man's need. But once again: this "existential" factor of theology must not be paraded at the expense of scientific exactitude. "In fact the strictest theology, that most passionately devoted to reality alone and ever on the alert for new questions, the most scientific theology, is itself in the long run the most kerygmatic."[3] Thus Rahner imposes on his students a task that is doubly hard: to deal with the content of theology in a strictly scientific way and at the same time always to face the question, "How shall I say this to the man in the street?" If the current theology of the schools provides no answer to this, Rahner treats it not only with contempt and irony, but also with anger.

It is also typical of Karl Rahner that he takes quite seriously the religious problem of man today, often understands it for the first time in its full import and brings all its consequences into the open. In the same spirit he is able to look at the Church and Christianity, as it were, from outside. He shows frankly and plainly what it is in the Church which makes it so difficult for non-Christians today to see in her a foundation of God himself. He sees

15

the consequence and lays his finger on it: non-Christians today will develop their own culture and morality in a reversal of the historical process.

> The non-Christian world, which (though we love to assert such things of it) is *not* a sheer mass of decomposition and deterioration, will even seek to develop its own forces, its own institutions of a social, intellectual, educational and moral kind, and these will certainly not be so obliging as to prove a mere series of desperate and unsuccessful efforts. These things will then make an impression on Christians, and refute our cheaply repetitious (and theologically false) propaganda to the effect that anywhere where the Church and the clergy are not in control and do not supply the principles of action, there can be nothing but disintegration and decay.[4]

Because of this honesty in analysis and language and because of his warning against all attempts to confine Christianity to the forms of pious associations, Rahner is regarded by some as a revolutionary. The description does not fit. His theology is just as traditional as it is original; he thinks at least as much with the Church, is quite as truly a man of the Church, as his critics. A frank way of speaking is natural to him, but so also is Ignatius of Loyola's whole-hearted and intimate devotion to the Church. Even when he speaks—as few before him have spoken—of the Church of sinners and the sinning Church, there is never the slightest doubt that he believes the same Church to be the infallible community of Jesus Christ ruled by the Spirit of God.

After this attempt to describe Karl Rahner's general outlook, we must now give a chronological account of his life. He is Swabian. He was born in Freiburg im Breisgau,

March 5, 1904. His parents also, Professor Karl Rahner (1868-1934) and Frau Luise Rahner (née Trescher, still living in Freiburg at the age of 90), came from that neighbourhood. People from these parts (Martin Heidegger, Karl Barth, Bernhard Welte, Max Müller, are among them) are supposed to be reserved, introspective, and ready to work like horses; they are considered to have a deep sense of humour, but no spontaneous and clear-sighted joy in life—only a melancholy irony. However that may be, Karl Rahner spent his youth from 1908-22 in Freiburg: he attended the boys' primary school 1910-13, the grammar school from 1913 until he gained his leaving certificate on March 29, 1922. There is not much to report about those early years. He was an average student, bored during lessons. He was an enthusiastic supporter of the youth movement and a member of "Quickborn".[5] Finally, he became friendly with Pier Giorgio Frassati. The latter was a young Italian student, born 1901, who lived with the Rahners and made a deep impression on Karl. How deep can be seen from his introduction in 1961 to Pier Giorgio's biography (he died of infantile paralysis in 1925):

> Even if there are now and were then many of his calibre, it would still be right to praise the young Christian as represented by Frassati: naturally radiant and virile, open to all that speaks of freedom and beauty, with a deep social sense, having at heart the Church and her destiny. But Frassati was more than this, as the reader ought to discover from this modern life of a saint. At that time there were not yet many who came from upper middle-class liberal circles and who also became Christians as Frassati did, without a trace of the usual psychological mechanism of the sons' protest against their fathers. That is the remark-

able thing: what he lacks is precisely this attitude of protest. He is a Christian simply by being there and his only protest consists in the fact that he assumes that this attitude, self-evident to him, is self-evident to everybody. He derives his courage and his power to be a Christian, not from his opposition to his parents' generation, not from cultural diagnoses and prognoses and the like, but from the Christian reality itself: that God is, that prayer is fruitful, that the sacraments nourish the "eternal in man", that all men are brothers. Here particularly the mysterious spontaneity of divine grace becomes perceptible: suddenly a Christian is again present where background and parents suggested that this was wholly a thing of the past. And he is happy simply to be, without adopting a party line and making an effort to be different. Here was a Christian who lived his Christianity as something which he accepted in an almost terrifying way as self-evident, with what to us seemed a dubious and maddening lack of problems (because he—although perhaps with tears —submerged the problems in the grace of faith): praying, eating the bread of death and life, loving his brethren.[6]

We may perhaps apply this catchword also to the youth and the decision of Karl Rahner: these were "self-evident". Self-evident, but as the result of a hard and stubbornly worked out decision which is not manifested by any external "conversion" and is proved by unceasing and selfless service.

On April 20, 1922, three weeks after his school-leaving examination, Karl Rahner entered the novitiate of the North German province of the Society of Jesus. It was then at Feldkirch in the Vorarlberg, in Austria. Three years earlier his brother, Hugo Rahner, had entered the same novitiate.[7] In the novitiate, he devoted himself completely to problems of the spiritual life, without ambitions, without expressing a preference for a particular field of activity: he was interested solely in the fundamentals of the religious life and the study of spiritual writers. He presented to the novitiate magazine the first drafts of some articles, wholly concerned with spirituality, which (as we shall see) later appeared in print.

On April 27, 1924, he took his vows as a scholastic (which in fact bind the religious to the Society of Jesus, but do not bind the Society to him). In accordance with the custom of the order, he spent the first year (1924-5) in studying philosophy at Feldkirch; the second and third year (1925-7) he spent at Pullach, near Munich. A stack of thick notebooks testifies to his industry during these years and reveals his special field of interest. His teachers in philosophy were then K. Frank, K. Frick, B. Jansen, J. B. Schuster, A. Willwoll: reputable and solid pedagogues. But there exists a further stack of notebooks, the evidence of his secret hobby. In these, in his clear, precise handwriting, Karl Rahner made excerpts from the works of Kant and of the Jesuit philosopher, J. Maréchal (d. 1944 in Louvain), who confronted thomism with Kantian philosophy and tried to make Kant's transcendental method fruitful for the thomist theory of knowledge.

During these first years of study, Karl Rahner's superiors in the Order must have intended him for a scholarly career: it seems that they were thinking of the history of philosophy. But, in accordance with the Jesuit rule, a period of practical work had to come before further intellectual formation, between philosophy and theology. For Rahner this consisted in giving Latin lessons in the juniorate in Feldkirch. It is certainly to this activity that he owes his astounding knowledge of Latin, shown in a variety of ways, both in the records of his principal Latin lectures in Innsbruck and in his speeches at the Council or in conversations with foreign theologians.

At that time one of his students was Alfred Delp, born 1907 in Mannheim, who became a Jesuit in 1926. Later he was associated with the monthly, *Stimmen der Zeit*, as sociologist, became one of the conspirators against Hitler, was arrested by the Nazis July 28, 1944, and was hanged in Berlin, February 2, 1945. The writings he left behind him have a right to rank among the modern "acts of the martyrs".[8] In 1938 we find him again as a close assistant of Karl Rahner.

Rahner began his theological studies in 1929 at Valkenburg in Holland. Among his teachers were outstanding scholars, some of them still living: K. Prümm, exegete and patrologist; J. Rabeneck and H. Lange, dogmatic theologians; H. Weisweiler, historian of dogma; F. Hürth, moral theologian; J. Grisar, church historian; E. Raitz von Prentz, ascetic theologian. On July 26, 1932, he was ordained priest in St Michael's church in Munich by Cardinal Faulhaber. His theological studies continued until 1933, after which he went for his tertianship—the year's retreat prescribed by the constitutions of the order —to St Andrä in the Lavant valley (Carinthia). In 1934 he was sent by his superiors to take a degree in philosophy at Freiburg, his birthplace.

For one with such innate gifts for the subject, the Freiburg faculty of philosophy at that time was a particularly interesting and stimulating centre. Normally, in the philosophical faculties and institutes, the student was not taught to philosophize, but instructed in the history of philosophy and restricted to the task of classifying philosophers, epochs, trends, etc. Together with Heidelberg, from 1890 onwards, Freiburg had the good fortune of receiving an uninterrupted succession of "real" philosophers of the so-called "Baden School" of Neo-Kantianism. In 1928 Martin Heidegger came to Freiburg: he had started out from Neo-Kantianism, but since 1927 had made his own radical way. There was, of course, a chair for Catholic philosophy, and this was occupied by Martin Honecker, a naïve, narrow-minded representative of that rationalistic neo-scholasticism which had little more to do with St Thomas Aquinas than had the bearded existentialists of Montmartre with the philosophy of existentialism. Rahner had to take his degree under Honecker's guidance; but as the prescriptions required him to study other subjects also for his doctorate, he was able to count among his real teachers two more well-known Freiburg scholars, the legal philosopher Erik Wolf and the historian Johannes Spörl. But Freiburg meant, above all, Martin Heidegger. Access to his famous seminar was not particularly easy. There Karl Rahner met Catholic students of Heidegger whose names are now everywhere famous: Gustav Siewerth, Bernhard Welte, Max Müller, Johannes B. Lotz, among others. He kept records also of these strenuous studies: notes on Heidegger's interpretation of Plato, Aristotle, Kant and the Pre-Socratics.

But the subject of a dissertation had to be settled with Honecker. It was to deal with thomistic epistemology: "thomistic" being understood here not in the sense of what we call thomism, not as the theories of commentators and imitators, but as the thought of Aquinas himself. Rahner wanted to write a philosophical, not an historical work. That also was the reason for choosing this theme: for Aquinas particularly the metaphysics of finite knowledge is the first approach to philosophical reflection, but —since he is essentially a theologian—it is nowhere completely and systematically worked out. Karl Rahner proves that in this approach the whole of Aquinas' teaching on human knowledge is contained and brought together in an original unity. Man's knowing takes place first and foremost in the world of experience, since the human mind is constantly turned towards the outward appearance. This principle Rahner develops systematically in his interpretation of Aquinas, starting out from the nature of the human question which man poses as soon as he appears in the world and asks about being as a whole. The consequences of this approach are far-reaching.

Being as knowing, occupied with a thing here and now, is called "sensation"; knowledge of being as a whole is called "intellect"; hence there must be a primal unity of both. Thus Aquinas also says that neither sensation nor intellect can ever be found as such in the concrete: the one can be distinguished from the other only in its unity with that other. Therefore the epistemological problem is not at all that of bridging the gap between knowing and object (this "gap" does not exist for Aquinas himself, but is a rationalistic pseudo-problem created by his interpreters): it is rather how the thing known, being identical with the knower, can be confronted with the knower and how therefore there can be any knowledge at all of another as such. From now onwards, Rahner works out this possibility from the fact that sensation originates in the mind—but we cannot follow the stages of this theory of knowledge here. An introduction to his life and work does not require an extensive treatment of this theme. It is sufficient to quote the closing sentences which indicate the point which Rahner has reached at the end of this inquiry:

> Aquinas as theologian is concerned with man as the point at which God shows himself in such a way that he can be heard in his revealing word: *ex parte*

animae. In order to be able to hear whether God is speaking, we must know that he is; in order that his word should not reach someone who already knows, he must be hidden from us. In order that he should speak to men, his word must reach us where we are always already present, at a point on earth, in earthly time. In so far as man enters into the world, by turning to the phantasm, being as such is always already revealed to him and in it he has already acquired a knowledge of the existence of God; but at the same time also this God always remains concealed as transcending this world. Abstraction is the disclosure of being as such, which places man before God; conversion is an entry into the here and now of this finite world, which makes God the distant Unknown. Abstraction and conversion for Aquinas are the same thing: man. If man is understood in this way, he can hear whether God perhaps is speaking, because he knows that God is; God can speak, because he is the Unknown. And if Christianity is not an idea of the eternal, ever-present spirit, but Jesus of Nazareth, Aquinas' epistemology is Christian in as much as it recalls man to the here and now of his finite world; for the Eternal also entered into it, in order that man should find him and in him once again find himself.[9]

Thus Rahner is right in the midst of the study or—we might say—appraisal of the first principles of theology. As Gottlieb Söhngen once very pointedly remarked, Catholic theology since Aquinas has been marking time on these questions. We have not seized on the suggestions provided by Aquinas himself: we preferred to work with the facts, not troubling to examine more closely the reason behind them. Within the scope of Catholic theology, the theme of fundamental theology ran: If

God reveals himself, man must attend; but God has revealed himself, naturally and supernaturally; therefore . . . This is no answer to the pressing questions of modern thought. Why is man able to hear God at all? How does such a reception of a divine revelation take place? More particularly, how can the hearer guarantee that it is a divine revelation and render a credible account of it to others? It was here that Rahner's theological road began: in the tracks of Aquinas; in conversation with Kant, with German Idealism, with Heidegger. The road led him to the elements of a Christian anthropology, a theological doctrine of man. And precisely by reflecting on "conversion", on man's necessary self-commitment to the world, there emerged for Rahner still further ideas essential for his theology: the positive valuation of earthly realities, the discovery of the importance of human time, the new appreciation of matrimony.

The conclusions to be drawn for epistemology, as also the whole vaster horizon thus revealed, were hidden from Martin Honecker. He reproached Rahner for taking up Aquinas' suggestions and then abandoning himself to the dynamism of their content. That was, and indeed remains, a fundamental problem: the question of interpretation, of understanding what an older philosopher really said and meant. Is Aquinas properly interpreted simply by grouping his statements in their original form as a, b, c, by the historical and sterile repetition of his axioms, as had hitherto been the practice of Martin Honecker or Hans Meyer in Germany? As we can see expressly stated in the preface to his work, Karl Rahner from the very beginning was quite clearly opposed to such a method, which does not do justice to real thinking: "If the reader thus gains the impression that this is an interpretation of Aquinas derived from modern philosophy, the author will consider such an observation as indicating not a defect but an advantage of the book: if only because he did not know why he should study Aquinas except for the sake of the questions which stir his philosophy and the philosophy of his time."[10] This of course was the very reason why Honecker refused to accept the work as a philosophical dissertation.

Rahner has never defended himself against Honecker, although it would have been easy for him to do so (it would have sufficed to publish his examiner's inept marginal comments on his dissertation[11]). The work was published by Felizian Rauch of Innsbruck in 1939, with the title, *Geist in Welt* (the foreword explains: "*Geist* is used as the name of a power that reaches beyond the world to grasp the metaphysical; *Welt* is the name of the reality accessible to man's immediate experience").[12] It was promptly described as an "extremely stimulating" book, written "with unusual speculative power: undoubtedly one of the most important books on scholastic philosophy to appear in recent times".[13] In 1957 Kösel-Verlag of Munich published a second edition of 414 pages, revised and augmented by Johannes Baptist Metz (who is certainly Rahner's most speculatively gifted student). No one then in Germany remembered the name of Honecker who had not wanted to grant Rahner his doctorate in philosophy, but about the same time Martin Heidegger made one of his rare journeys in order to pay a visit to his now famous student in Innsbruck.

Before following his career further, we must take a side-glance at Rahner. He has a spontaneous inclination towards pastoral care for the individual, the renewal and deepening of faith: his sermons draw men, not through a display of rhetoric, but because he reads the hearer's secret and open questions as in a book, gives them expression and makes them his own—even if at the end all that remains is a question about the mystery of God and no ready-made recipes have been thundered out. Rahner's sermons are marked by the greatest respect for the individual person as hearer: he has never played upon those instincts which can very easily be roused in any large audience; he has never talked for the sake of talking. In brief: he is by nature what is conventionally called "a spiritual director", of the kind that Ignatius of Loyola would have wanted as director of the Exercises; he is particularly concerned with the human mind (not to be understood in a rationalist sense) and with calling it to real contemplation, but he is inclined to neglect the aesthetic aspect of things. I mention all this here because, at the time of which we are speaking, in Freiburg about the year 1934, he was invited for the first time to give retreats. From that time onwards, he has never refused such requests provided he could somehow snatch time for them.[14]

He returned in 1936 from Freiburg to Innsbruck. At the wish of his superiors he prepared himself for a doctorate in theology, writing a dissertation (still unpublished) on the Church's origin from the wound in the side of Christ as portrayed in the writings of the Fathers: as a result of this, he became doctor of theology at Innsbruck (December 19, 1936). He was expected soon to begin teaching at the university, an appointment that was not difficult to obtain under the laws then prevailing in Austria, provided the candidate could show that he had already published learned works. In fact, he had published in 1932-4 the articles on spiritual theology originally written for the novitiate magazine: in the French *Revue d'Ascétique et de Mystique*, there appeared "Cinq sens spirituels chez Origène" (1932), "Les sens spirituels au Moyen-Age, en particulier chez Bonaventure" (1933) and "Coeur de Jésus chez Origène" (1934); in *Zeitschrift für Aszese und Mystik*, "Die geistliche Lehre des Evagrius Ponticus" (1933) and "Der Begriff Ecstasis bei Bonaventura" (1934). These were accepted and he was appointed to the theological faculty at the university of Innsbruck on July 1, 1937, and in the winter term of that year began his lectures on dogmatic theology.

What was unique in Rahner's theology lay mainly in the continuation of the line of thought begun in Freiburg: his is a metaphysical, not a positive historical theology. Negatively, this means that it contains neither "leaps" nor "twists" and thus that any particular development can be traced back to the "origin".

This first became clear in 1937 at the Salzburg summer-school, when Rahner gave fifteen lectures on "the Foundation of a Philosophy of Religion". These were later worked up into a book, *Hörer des Wortes*, published in 1941. A new edition of this important work, revised by J. B. Metz, appeared in 1963.[15] He is concerned here, not with a "scientific-theoretical" foundation of the philosophy of religion as a branch of theology, but with the objective, basic question of man's relationship to God: whether and how man is positively open to a divine revelation, without there being any necessity that this revelation should take place. The question therefore is metaphysical and not yet definitely theological, but it arises precisely out of the common ground of philosophy (of religion) and theology in which the nature of man himself is in question. Man is spirit, but spirit in space and time. He can be spirit, therefore, only when he applies himself to the phenomenon. To *a* phenomenon? To the greatest possible abundance of phenomena. For the richer and more varied are these phenomena, the more there appears in them the goal of the human spirit: "being as such, that also extends beyond this world".[16] But at the same time man is himself phenomenon, the most spiritual of phenomena. In him, therefore, being as such can also reach its fullest expression. This in fact takes place at the point where man's being is most completely realized. For Rahner that is above all the history of mankind. If absolute, infinite being were not to speak at all, it would still be present, and the most essential thing about human history would then be God's silence in it. But the history of mankind remains the point at which God may possibly speak and man in his innermost nature is the one who listens to the word of God or awaits God's self-disclosure. "Only one who hears in this way is what he really has to be: man."[17] That is how Karl Rahner attempts to define man: "the being of receptive spirituality standing in freedom before God, who is free in regard to a possible revelation: a revelation which, if it occurs, takes on the form of a word spoken in man's history."[18] So far human thought can reach. To elaborate it, is the function of theology, attending in faith to the content of the word thus uttered.

"God's communication of himself to man" thus became a kind of summary of Karl Rahner's theology of grace, on which he lectured in Innsbruck from 1937 onwards. For him this central point of Christian dogmatic theology gains its character from his basic reflections on man as constantly open, attentive, and on God as freely and without any necessity communicating himself to man: that is, from his anthropology. Furthermore, it bears the imprint of a sound and thoroughgoing biblical theology and of a special understanding of patristic theology, above all of the Greek Fathers (in which Rahner made use of modern French studies in patrology, particularly of the work of Henri de Lubac and Jean Daniélou), and finally of a broad presentation of the Tridentine teaching on justification. In all these points

Rahner's text on the Catholic theology of grace, which he composed in Latin and in that winter of 1937 had duplicated for the use of his students, is quite different from the usual text-book treatment. This *Codex de Gratia* was four times expanded and appeared with 350 pages in 1954 at Innsbruck. Out of this intense preoccupation with the theology of grace there also resulted a number of important articles: in the history of theology, the essays on the concept of the "supernatural" in Clement of Alexandria (in the Roman review, *Gregorianum*, 1937), on Augustine and Semi-Pelagianism (in *Zeitschrift für katholische Theologie*, 1938), and on the scholastic conception of uncreated grace (*ibid.*, 1939); in systematic theology, the essay on the theological concept of concupiscence (*ibid.*, 1941).

Something really ought to be said here about the situation of theology generally in those years just before the outbreak of war. I shall try to do this in the second part of the book. For it is only in the light of that situation that we can understand why Rahner has raised so many and such varied theological problems. But there is one aspect that may be mentioned now. Those who belonged to that generation of theologians, then thirty to forty years old, were trying with all their mind and heart to break free from the sad state to which Catholic theology had been reduced. Some wished to free theology from the rigidity which had been caused by the severity of the Roman reaction to heretical modernism, and also to the youthful biblical movement, to Herman Schell, to the liturgical renewal and to inter-confessional discussion (we may recall the banishment of Dom Lambert Beauduin in Belgium). (From one point of view this rigidity could be excused, for there seemed nothing left now to do except to repeat what had already been said constantly for 400 years.) On the other hand, there were some who though wanting to remain Catholic, had set themselves apart from the Church and her teaching office and had published a number of books under pseudonyms and without *imprimatur*, attacking the state of affairs at the time.

Midway between these fronts was a group of young theologians who did not wish to adopt either attitude. As theologians and teachers in the Church, they wanted again to enter into conversation, to discuss; they wanted to bring to an end heresy-hunting and meddling behind the scenes in ecclesiastical politics. As in French theology, they emphasized the importance of friendly co-operation (rejecting professorial high-handedness and trying to meet the needs of the time): they wanted to engage in team work. First of all, Hugo Rahner must be mentioned in this connection: he was professor of early Church history and of patrology in Innsbruck from 1935 and co-operated at that time with his brother Karl on the content (but not on the scientific theory) of a "kerygmatic theology".[19] In Munich, also working in this direction, was a group of theologians which consisted of A. Delp, P. Bolkovac, H. Urs von Balthasar, A. Lieske (all Jesuits), and in Freiburg, Dr Robert Scherer. In 1938 Karl Rahner also joined this group. Particularly important was the new scheme of dogmatic theology which he drew up with the assistance of von Balthasar and which later appeared in the first volume of his *Schriften zur Theologie*.[20] At this time also the idea was conceived of a series of works, *Quaestiones Disputatae*, reviving from the great ages of Catholic theology a tradition of discussion and enquiry.

At first, this work had no outward success. In March 1938 National-Socialist Germany invaded Austria. The Nazis quickly exploited the initial enthusiasm of the Austrians and the cultural inferiority of the Austrian Catholics, interfering with the Church much more than they had done in Germany itself. On July 20, 1938, they abolished the theological faculty of the university of Innsbruck. The professors continued their teaching in the building of the Jesuit college, where it was possible for a while to maintain the normal life of the order and the daily routine. On August 15, 1939, Rahner made his final vows in the order, taking his vows as a professed religious in the Austrian Jesuit novitiate at St Andrä in the Lavant valley (Carinthia).

In October 1939 the Jesuit college in Innsbruck was closed by the Nazis. War had by now been declared and in Germany they were preaching loyalty to the "Führer, Volk und Vaterland". Rahner received a "district prohibition" (*Gauverbot*) and was sent away from the Tyrol. The Viennese prelate, Karl Rudolf, as the Cardinal's delegate, offered him refuge in Vienna and took him into the diocesan administration (with the title of "curial counsellor") and into the pastoral institute. In his book, *Aufbau im Widerstand* (an account of pastoral work in Austria 1938-45), Rudolf describes the courageous efforts of this Viennese group against the Nazis, the fearless way in which they continued their theological and pastoral activities, and in particular brings out the value of Karl Rahner's contribution.[21] His lectures, especially in the pastoral institute and in the church of the Friars Minor, were concerned with anthropology as the point of departure for theology and with the philosophy of Martin Heidegger (even in 1940, the Paris review, *Recherches de science religieuse*, published Rahner's article on this subject, "An Introduction to Heidegger's Conception of Existentialist Philosophy"); but they also formed complete courses of dogmatic theology and seminars on particular questions, on questions of asceticism and mysticism, on sexual ethics and other problems of the layman in the Church. In spite of the dangerous situa-

Karl Rahner

tion, Rahner left Vienna, from 1939 to 1944, to lecture in Leipzig, Dresden, Strasbourg and Cologne. In this way a foundation was established for many later publications, additional stones to be built into the structure of a modern dogmatic theology following the Munich outline.

One thing that happened during the years that Rahner spent in Vienna deserves to be recalled (it is published here for the first time). On January 18, 1943, Conrad Gröber, then archbishop of Freiburg, issued a letter of twenty-one pages addressed to the German (and Austrian) episcopate. In this letter (which lies before me, together with the rest of the material), the archbishop complains bitterly of innovations "in the field of Catholic theology and liturgy", which he sums up in seventeen points:

1. The division within the clergy between old and young (among the reckless young were included also the "liturgical agitators", the supporters of a "kerygmatic theology", the "Viennese activists", who "rush to adopt the new schemes and in the light of these to reorganize their parishes").

2. The decline of interest in natural theology.

3. A new definition of faith (the conception of faith as "becoming conscious of unity with Christ" and other similar ideas).

4. The increasing depreciation of scholastic philosophy and theology.

5. The bold and reckless reversion in practice to early and primitive times, norms and forms.

6. The one-sided preference for the Eastern Fathers, "with their peculiar ideas and forms of expression".

7. The increasing influence of Protestant dogmatic theology on the Catholic presentation of the faith.

8. Throwing open the frontiers in relation to other

Churches in order to fulfil the aims of the *Una Sancta* movement.

9. The modern concept of the Church, "according to which it is no longer the *societas perfecta*, founded by Christ, but a kind of 'biological organism'."

10. The excessive supernaturalism and the new mystical attitude in our theology.

11. The Christ-mysticism, "now flourishing, which I do not know whether to describe as astonishing or shocking".

12. The conclusions drawn from the doctrine of the mystical body of Christ ("people really seem to be forgetting that metaphors such as St Paul uses must not be overworked, but must be explained . . . in the light of the fact—which certainly holds also for St Paul—that all comparisons limp").

13. Over-emphasis on the universal priesthood.

14. The thesis of the meal-sacrifice and the sacrificial meal ("the communion of the faithful is supposed to belong to the integrity, if not to the essence, of the Mass, the practice of primitive Christianity being invoked to support this; it is forgotten that in fact, even then, on special occasions and in special conditions, Holy Communion was also received outside Mass").

15. Over-emphasis on the liturgy ("I hold, and many share my opinion, that pastoral work went on quite efficiently before an appreciation of the liturgy spread to wider circles").

16. The attempt to make dialogue Mass compulsory ("I shall always regard dialogue Mass merely as a peripheral and temporary phenomenon").

17. The attempt to conciliate the people by introducing the German language even in the Mass (the archbishop considers the adoption of the mother-

tongue for the Mass "a loosening of the spiritual bonds with the Church and with Rome itself").

Archbishop Gröber closes his letter with the question, "Can we—the bishops of all Germany—and can Rome remain silent any longer on these matters?"

It would be unjust to criticize this document today in the light of the encyclical on the mystical body, published shortly afterwards in June 1943, in the light of the encyclical on the liturgy, *Mediator Dei* in 1947, or finally from the standpoint of the splendid prospects set before us by Vatican Council II. The document itself was forgotten in the breakdown of the "Third Reich". But it had an effect, which is of great interest here, in connection with the life and work of Karl Rahner. Cardinal Innitzer of Vienna commissioned his pastoral institute to draw up a full refutation: it was in fact composed by Rahner, and went to fifty-three pages. Some of the items from this unpublished Viennese memorandum are reproduced here.

A preliminary observation points out that the Freiburg complaints relate to changes brought about by time which could not have been avoided and should never be delayed. "Just as the Church in earlier times, in her language, in the development of worship, in emphasizing and bringing out particular truths of faith, in her art, in the forms of her organization (so far as these are determined by variable, human, ecclesiastical law), in the concrete practices of the religious life—in all these things—naturally lived by the life of that age, so the Church today also lives into our own age. Since she has the promise of enduring to the end of time, we know she will do this also at all times and everywhere. For all that, this is a task which human beings in the Church at different times accomplish more or less well: they may, indeed, fail completely in this task in particular countries." The danger is clearly indicated of such failure leading to estrangement of the younger generation from the Church. But after that the problem is considered more deeply: "It is only when there is an honest attempt at finding new ways and means that the will to maintain tradition is likely to be effective also in the future."

"There is no reason for being disturbed by the fact that new life is everywhere stirring, or that the problems and tasks of the age are perceived and discussed, and that new ways are opened and tried. Nor need we be disturbed if this initiative is not simply stimulated by orders and directives from above, but comes out spontaneously from below. A leadership which found such a spontaneous initiative of its followers unwelcome and disturbing would thereby betray only its own uncertainty and incapacity to guide and rule a really living Church. Neither dogmatic theology nor Church history provide any evidence that the great vital movements in the Church of God, by which she meets again the needs of each new age, have always to be started by the hierarchy itself." These words closely recall what Pius XII said a few months later about the laity receiving their special charisms in the Church and for the Church.

Rahner then shows how valuable discussions are in the Church. "But in all the heat of debate mutual charity must constantly be maintained. Even when we differ on a particular question, we must still recognize always that the other person's efforts are also inspired by a real love of the Church and genuine concern for her future. Here particularly, unjust generalizations inflict wounds and create bitterness." He raises the question which is still, and indeed must ever remain, urgent in the Church: "If all those who assume that such charges and warnings are addressed to themselves were to withdraw from the

Church's life and letters into silence, could this loss be borne?"

He also gives practical advice: "If the complaint is raised that the ordinary parochial clergy scarcely know their way any longer in the confusion of opinions, then we must respond by urging that greater efforts be made to provide for the priest's further training by using lectures, courses, study-days and so on." This, in fact, was done after the war.

The right to appeal to the earlier ages of the Church is similarly asserted, but its limitations are noted. "For in no particular age, taken in isolation, does the Church show forth in her teaching and deeds, without reserve and with equal explicitness, the whole fullness of truth and reality bestowed on her by Christ: so we can always appeal to the Church of an earlier age or to an earlier phase in the history of theology when the very thing that we regard as necessary and useful for the situation in our own time was more clearly manifested than in the immediate past."

Rahner examines closely the state of Catholic theology in Germany at that time. The great names and achievements of historical theology are noted. But: "We are not too richly blessed with great synthetic works making the results of research into the history of dogma available to the average student, which can be turned to account for the real work of dogmatic theology. . . . What is a person to do now if he wants to read a history of dogma? Has he any alternative but to take up Harnack or, better, Seeberg? We have no compendium of biblical theology, we have no history of scholastic theology, we have no history of modern theology, we have no large Catholic history of religion, we have no history of moral theology."

Rahner never ceases to insist that scientific theology

36

must remain exact: theologians cannot have it handed to them, but must reach their conclusions as a result of persistent hard work. He speaks of the many good text-books in German and Latin, but points out that these provide only a basis for a real study of theology: "These text-books rightly offer the traditional teaching. But theological life with its new questionings, problems, notably in its contact with the whole modern attitude and way of thinking, and living, in Germany does not, as we might perhaps expect, express itself first in the form of strictly scientific studies: mainly and almost exclusively it is expressed in more popular writings directed to wider circles and, therefore, rightly avoiding precise definitions and closely reasoned theological argument (we may mention, for example, Peter Lippert, Romano Guardini, Eugen Walter). For all that, this phenomenon of a theological forward movement outside professional theological circles carries with it an element of danger: first, there is the danger of these hints not being properly appreciated by and embodied in the self-satisfied text-book theology; and so in the long run they will not be sufficiently far-reaching in their effects; . . . then, if the young student of theology is pressed with new questions, he tries to find an answer for himself and others on a plane which more easily permits the provisional, the non-committal, mere 'essays' and the like." He takes a glance across the frontiers: "If we may judge from the number and extent of their learned works, the French clergy appear to be bolder and more industrious in their writing and more ready to make sacrifices in order to buy books."

Even at that time, Rahner was concerned about exegesis and its relation to dogmatic theology.[22] "We perhaps cannot entirely avoid the impression that in some places the courage and confidence to venture into

37

the sphere of exegesis on delicate, but also important and urgent questions of dogmatic theology, is not yet great enough. Severe measures on the part of the Church might indeed prevent blunders, but they could also have the unhappy result of causing these questions to be left untouched through fear of conflict with ecclesiastical authority; exegesis would be applied more or less exclusively to harmless themes, by-passing more pressing problems in this field. . . . In Germany we have no sort of large scholarly commentaries either on the Old or on the New Testament, which might make us at least independent scientifically of Protestant exegesis, . . . no theology of the New Testament, no theological dictionary of the New Testament, no manual concordance."

Afterwards, he deals with a number of individual questions raised by the Freiburg letter.

Kerygmatic theology: This he rejects completely as a science in itself, but "The average student seems unable to discover the way to live preaching from dogmatic theology as it is often taught in the colleges".

Eastern theology: "Eastern theology will always have something fresh to say to the West, as it gave new inspiration to Aquinas, Petavius and Scheeben. The theology of the East on the Resurrection and Transfiguration, on worship, on the unity of asceticism and mysticism, on symbols, and on the transfiguration of the whole cosmos through grace, can even today give a new impulse to our Western theology."

The doctrine of grace and Christ-mysticism: "At a time when man's external social and cultural ties with Christianity and the Church are in practice more or less completely broken, and when an ethical idealism is propagated even by unbelievers, the Christian can in the long run maintain his faith only by living quite consciously on what is at the very heart of Christian existence, namely, his supernatural deifying union through grace with the triune God through the Mediator Jesus Christ."

Liturgical renewal: "Since what is meant by the term 'Catholic Action' even today—and, in fact, to the highest degree—retains its importance, and as the task of the laity which it implies can be fulfilled only if they live by the power of Christ's sacrifice, the greatest possible inward and the clearest possible outward participation of the laity in the sacrifice of Christ in the Church is of fundamental importance."

Summarizing this first part, Rahner concludes that there really is no need for prohibitions and warnings from the highest ecclesiastical authorities, but there are certainly many occasions for positively promoting theological activity. He mentions a renewal of the intellectual formation of theological students, the further training of the clergy in theology, the encouragement of theological students and scholarly work by the bishops and not only by the faculties, literary planning and promotion of greater works by the episcopate. "It is by stimulating forces that one can best direct them. When all the resources are positively and confidently called upon, applied to given tasks with all that is necessary to achieve them, they are most easily directed in an orderly fashion to their goal. Only by seeking boldly a new future ourselves shall we maintain in the long run what is indispensable from the past and gain also a future for it."

Rahner devoted thirty-four pages of the memorandum to this stock-taking and programme-making of theology. The remaining nineteen pages concern philosophy. This cannot be discussed here with the same thoroughness. But one quotation may be permitted. "Modern philosophy also has its series of classical figures (Descartes, Leibniz, Kant, Fichte, Schelling, Hegel, Schopenhauer,

Nietzsche, Kierkegaard) whose thought, arising from the intellectual divisions of modern times, is so original, vital and deep that a live contact with them is an indispensable requirement for a living Christian philosophy today. This does not mean any sort of immediate outward adoption even of a single point, but a vital contact with these philosophers compels the Christian philosopher constantly to develop his own system afresh and from its roots; he must break down again and again every rigid text-book formula that is merely handed on from the past and cut out all verbalism: in this way he will always see afresh the eternally new similarity of problems here and there and thus learn how to translate the language of one philosophy into that of the other."

For Rahner's biography, it is interesting that—as this Viennese memorandum shows—he is not merely a speculative theologian, given to clear analysis, but has practical ideas and suggestions also. He does not waste time on individual problems, but keeps in mind the grand "strategy" of the Church. We need only glance at the present situation to see how much of his programme has since been realized. But his suggestions for reforming theological studies have been too little noticed. I may therefore be permitted again to quote some of his remarks on this subject:

Academic teaching is teaching with the object of making someone, within its special subject, capable, in terms of learning and training, of taking his place among those who are working to advance that subject. It is this goal, and this alone, that distinguishes a university from a school for advanced specialists. Because of this, there have to be, of course, as many specialists in a university as there are lines of advance in research, determined by the respective subjects "*in themselves*" and differentiated according to subject and method. Now, the academic teaching in the theological faculties of the universities is going to be done academically in this sense (no matter what modifications and omissions may be imposed by lack of time and the good sense of professors with a personal ideal of education focused on the priesthood). In itself this is an acceptable way to do it. For there has to be theological research, and hence academic training for it. But is it something for the great mass of theological students, who want to be and are to be priests later on, and not the next generation of theological research workers?

The identification between the training of a pastoral priest and of a scholarly theologian must be abolished. . . . The goal to be aimed at in the theology provided for future priests and pastors will have to involve a lightening, a concentration, and a deepening of the course of studies in comparison with what has been in use heretofore.

Lightening: We can spare the theological student a great deal of what is, for him, superfluous ballast of learned material, which he cannot really master nor make any use of later on. Obviously, a man whose abilities are both above average and, as to their quality, of a specifically *scholarly* nature, can make use later on, even in pastoral work, what he has acquired earlier in the course of his learned studies. But the abilities of the majority are not above average, and in still fewer, today, are they specifically scholarly (rational and analytical). . . .

Concentration: The existing mass of special subjects should be pulled together and regrouped from points of view that are priestly and related to pastoral practice; these need to be thought out precisely and radically. It ought to be clear that not everything that a future

41

priest has to learn need necessarily be communicated
to him by formal teaching (an obvious principle, constantly contradicted in practice). . . .

Deepening: If theology keeps its eyes resolutely
fixed on the goal of giving today's priests and pastors
what they need, then it will appear, perhaps very
quickly, that this goal cannot of course be reached by
giving a cut-down version of "scientific" theology as
it has been hitherto. Rather, it will be seen that theology (dogmatic and moral especially) needs in many
respects to be deepened, so that it can be given to
theological students in the way in which they need it.
It is, for instance, or no use (or very little use) for a
future pastor to have acquired merely the formal
framework of concepts, the facts and proofs of the
history of dogma, taught to him out of theological
sources. He cannot, when the time comes, preach that.[23]

Rahner's programme of a training for specialist theologians distinct from that given to the parochial clergy
has never, so far as I know, been adopted, although the
outline was sent with the Viennese memorandum to all
the appropriate authorities.

In summer 1944, his public activity in Vienna was
over. As the Russians advanced nearer to the city, the
terror of the SS increased. Rahner had to leave Vienna.
In July 1944, he came to a small village in Lower Bavaria
and there took over the pastoral care of the local people
and many refugees. After the entry of the Americans, he
was called in August 1945 to the Jesuit college of St
John Berchman in Pullach, near Munich, where the
study of theology had just been resumed. There he taught
dogmatic theology and also did a great deal of work in
the badly bombed city of Munich. In 1946, a year of
hunger and distress, he preached the Lenten sermons in
St Michael's Church on "Need and Blessing in Prayer".

which were published as a book two years later by Felizian Rauch of Innsbruck. Much as I admire Rahner as a professional theologian, I feel compelled to describe this book, together with his small prayerbook, *Words into Silence*, as the best and most influential part of his work: for, in the last resort, what is learning by comparison with the realization of God in the heart of the individual and solitary human being?

In Munich also from 1945 to 1948 he covered five times the whole range of Catholic dogmatic theology in courses of lectures for interested adults. In August 1948, he returned to Innsbruck, where the theological faculty had been restored, and took over from his predecessor, F. Mitzka, the latter's dogmatic courses: a three-year cycle covering creation and original sin, grace, justification, faith, hope and charity, Penance, Anointing of the Sick and Holy Orders. On June 30, 1949, he was officially appointed as university professor and soon afterwards nominated as a member of the philosophical society of Louvain. He returned to Munich recently, having been appointed in November 1963 by the Bavarian Ministry of Culture to take the chair previously occupied by Romano Guardini: the title is "Philosophy of Religion and Catholic Weltanschauung" and the course is in the philosophical faculty of the university. Rahner came to live in Munich in spring 1964 and began his lectures in May.

His career as a publicist began properly with the appointment to Innsbruck in 1949. First of all, there should be mentioned the duplicated scripts of his three courses in dogmatic theology: the first, on grace, has been described above; the second script (likewise, almost a complete manual), on the doctrine of creation and original sin, was produced in 1950 (second edition, 1955, with 298 pages); the third and longest deals with the history and theology of the sacrament of Penance, first appearing at Pullach as early as 1946 (fourth edition, 785 pages, Innsbruck, 1960). Solid studies on the history and theology of the sacrament of Penance also appeared one after another in *Zeitschrift für katholische Theologie*: on Penance in Irenaeus (1949), in the Didascalia (1950), in Cyprian (1952) and in the "Shepherd" of Hermas (1955); in *Recherches de science religieuse* he wrote on Penance in Origen (1950); to a *Festschrift* for Karl Adam he contributed a study of Penance in Tertullian (if this last work were published, it would provide a survey of the sacrament of Penance in all its aspects).

The many lectures which Rahner has given since the situation in Europe became normal must also be mentioned. It is impossible to enumerate them all, but the fact deserves to be stressed that he spoke at a conference of Catholic and Protestant theologians for the first time in 1948 in Bad Driburg, Westphalia, and that he has been an active member of this body ever since. It meets annually under the patronage of the local evangelical bishop and the archbishop of Paderborn, and is the prototype of the secretariat for promoting the unity of Christians, set up in Rome in 1960, drawing some of its members from the German group. One of the most prominent participants, Hermann Volk, a friend of Rahner, became Bishop of Mainz in 1962. During these years, Rahner has spoken before retreat-givers, superiors of religious orders and abbots, doctors and psychiatrists, youth-chaplains, publicists and sociologists, before teachers and university people of all kinds; he has spoken at pastoral conferences, at family associations and adult educational organizations; he has addressed philosophical societies in Innsbruck and Berne, the German liturgical commission, the study-group of *Lumen Vitae* (Brussels) and has visited for similar purposes Merano, Bolzano, Zürich, Maastricht, the abbey of Mont-César in Louvain, Trent, Basle, Haarlem, Nijmegen, West and East Berlin, Comillas, Granada, Hilversum, Salzburg, Hanover. He has been guest-lecturer at the universities of Würzburg, Bonn, Nijmegen, Heidelberg, at the Pontifical Gregorian University and the Pontifical Biblical Institute in Rome, and in many priests' seminaries. Since 1948 also he has given over a hundred radio addresses on more than a dozen wave-lengths, and has made some appearances on television.

At first, these enterprises, absorbing much time and energy, seemed to have no clear direction. The themes were suggested by the needs of the moment and were freshly prepared on each occasion: any one of them might be a part of the structure of a universal dogmatic theology as it ought to be. They belong to the scope of what I have called in the second part of this little book "the diversity and multiplicity of theological problems". In this sense Rahner has no "life's work" on which he is silently and unremittingly engaged. But for a number of years two groups of themes have been coming to the fore which are outside this field.

Since the Goerres Society set up a branch to deal with the relations between theology and natural science, Rahner has been one of its members and has taken an active part in its annual meetings. His work, for instance, on the question of hominization belongs to this sphere: [24] it is one which has first of all to be discussed between theology and natural science, but which also carries implications for a future confrontation of theology with atheistic materialism. In 1962 the Pauline Society (*Paulus-Gesellschaft*) appeared for the first time in public. It had come into being through the initiative of Dr Erich Kellner and the inspiration of the university professors, Paul Martini in Bonn and Hans Schaefer in Heidelberg. From the beginning Karl Rahner has been the theological partner in this discussion with scholars representing the natural sciences and the arts: they have made Salzburg their centre. The basis here is broader than in the Goerres Society and the problem is to reach an understanding between two ways of thinking and speaking which are more deeply estranged from one another than people in the Church think possible. The esteem in which Rahner is held in this group was shown spontaneously in summer 1962, when 250 German university professors (none of them theologians) gave written expression to their feeling.

The second group of themes may be described as "The relations between Christianity and the non-Christian religions".[25] Here also Rahner envisages a problem which cannot be avoided by the Church of the future.

All this had at least to be mentioned, since it is characteristic of Rahner's open-mindedness towards the world of today. Other items might have been added—for instance, his contacts with Erik von Kühnelt-Leddihn, Walter Dirks, Luise Rinser, Heinrich Böll, or the intense pleasure he takes in ultra-modern art—but this must suffice.

Something further must be said of the work undertaken by Rahner which has now appeared in print. The two first post-war projects required considerable industry and care for detail which had never been properly appreciated. From its twenty-eighth to its thirty-first edition (Herder, Barcelona, 1958), he improved and augmented Denzinger's *Enchiridion Symbolorum*, a collection of texts of the Church's official teaching from the earliest professions of faith to the present time, which is an indispensable source-book for theological studies.[26] Rahner also undertook some of the later editions of what amounted to a German Denzinger, with the documents arranged under subject-headings instead of in chronological order, *Der Glaube der Kirche in den Urkunden der Lehrverkündigung*, first edited by the Jesuits, J. Neuner and H. Roos (sixth edition, 1961, Pustet, Regensburg); this was obviously meant to be of particular use to lay persons studying theology.

After the war, Robert Scherer often turned to Rahner to discuss with him larger theological projects. We can trace back to these discussions two important theological works which Rahner had already suggested in his Viennese memorandum. One is a manual of the history of dogma, planned for five volumes, of which instalments have been appearing since 1951;[27] the other is a learned commentary on the New Testament of which three volumes have appeared since 1953. In addition to these two projects, Herder was anxious to keep up particularly its century-old tradition of theological dictionaries. The *Lexikon für Theologie und Kirche*, which appeared in ten large volumes between 1930-8, is naturally out of date on most points. Discussions about a new edition began in 1955 with Professor Oskar Köhler, the intention at first being to invite Rahner and his followers to contribute a number of longer articles. The draft produced by Rahner of the whole Lexicon (which was not, however, realized in its entirety), was so promising that he was asked to undertake the editorship in collaboration with Monsignor Josef Höfer (Rome). The work began to appear in 1957 under the patronage of the Archbishop of Freiburg and the Bishop of Regensburg. The ten volumes planned (each with about 1340 columns) have now appeared.[28] In more than 30,000 articles all aspects of theology and the Church are covered, together with a great variety of related topics, from Aristotle to symbolic logic, from the Stock Exchange to artificial insemination. Among the 2,400 contributors are cardinals, bishops, abbots and nearly all Catholic scholars of repute; but there are also leading contemporary Protestant and Anglican scholars. A third of the contributors are from outside Germany. We can appreciate something of the labour in which Rahner is involved in the planning and execution of this work (including proof-reading at various stages). The great success of this Lexicon shows it is appreciated for being not only a primary source of information, but also a send-off to the twenty-first century.

While working on this Lexicon, Rahner began to take up the old idea of *Quaestiones Disputatae* and planned with Herder the publication of a series of theological monographs in which themes would be presented for discussion and then left to the theologians to develop. In the preface to the first of these we read:

> Anything that a human being as a Christian might want to clarify in his own mind could find a place in this series, on the sole condition that this clarification is made with that relevance and conceptual exactitude which makes a reflection into a learned study. If we can keep the size of the individual work to reasonable limits, we may perhaps also hope that these studies, without loss to their specialist character, will find a rather wider circle of readers than merely among specialist scholars. If we succeed in helping the priest in his pastoral work to maintain a really vital contact with theology, in certain conditions also help the oft-quoted layman to find the hint of an answer to his frequently really pressing theological problems, then this would be a more pleasing result to us than the tribute of purely theological scholarship.[29]

The co-editor of this series is Heinrich Schlier; since 1957 over twenty-eight titles have appeared, several of which have already been translated into other languages.

In 1953, Dr Oscar Bettschart, director of Benzinger-Verlag in Einsiedeln, urged Karl Rahner to collect together his more important articles, spread about in various reviews, and publish them in a series of volumes. As a result, there appeared from 1954 onwards the *Schriften zur Theologie*, of which there are now six volumes containing over a hundred articles.[30] A similar collection of twenty-four articles, of a more practical and contemporary character, appeared for the first time in 1959, published by Tyrolia, Innsbruck, under the title of *Sendung und Gnade* (*Mission and Grace*).[31]

Rahner recorded for the first time in 1960 meditations on Advent, Christmas, Good Friday and Holy Saturday. These are included in the collection of sermons for the Church's year, published in Germany under the title *Kleines Kirchenjahr*, and in England and America as *The Eternal Year*.[32] Further records are being produced.

In 1961, Karl Rahner and I spent a summer holiday in writing a *Kleines theologisches Wörterbuch* (published in England and America under the title, *A Concise Dictionary of Theology*[33]), wholly, as was natural, from the standpoint of Rahner's theology. Under more than 600 headings we have tried to face and—as far as possible—answer the main problems of dogmatic theology.

In 1962, we edited a six-hundred-page symposium, *Diaconia in Christo*, in which we solicited contributions from an international group of thirty-three writers, on the important question of the revival of the diaconate (more will be said about this in the second part of this book). The work was undertaken expressly in view of the Council and its pastoral aims—for a permanent, married diaconate appears to be the only practical solution to the problems arising from the catastrophic shortage of priests in some parts of the world. At this time Rahner was already very much occupied with preparation

49

for the Council and had written several hundred pages of expert comment on its projects.

"In spare time"—so to speak—he went on with his plans for the future. He prepared the basic outline for a manual of pastoral theology, the first volume of which was published by Herder in 1964. It is the work of a team consisting of Karl Rahner, F. X. Arnold (Tübingen), V. Schurr (Gars and Rome) and L. M. Weber (Solothurn). Considerable progress has also been made on a kerygmatic lexicon, *Sacramentum Mundi*, to be published by Herder. It will appear simultaneously in German (ed. Karl Rahner), French (ed. J. Daniélou), Spanish (ed. J. Alfaro), Italian (ed. C. Colombo), and English[34] (ed. M. O'Connell, S.J. and C. Ernst, O.P.), and perhaps also in Dutch: intended particularly as an aid to the parochial clergy and to preachers, it will be kept free from all unnecessary ballast. Finally, two well-known Swiss theologians, J. Feiner and M. Löhrer, O.S.B., are planning for Benziger-Verlag a manual of theology based on Rahner's outline course of dogma, but including also biblical and moral theology. This will be called *Mysterium Salutis* and will also appear simultaneously in several languages,[35] the contributors including Rahner's students and friends. The first volume is almost ready.

Together with Edward Schillebeeckx, O.P., and other distinguished theologians, Rahner helped to launch the international theological review, *Concilium*, of which the first issue appeared in six languages in January 1965.

This completes the main outline of Rahner's work up to the present time: some of the prospects for the future have been indicated. It is, of course, obvious that so tremendous an achievement with such vast horizons, emerging from so personal a temperament, was bound to rouse strong but justifiable opposition, as well as envious polemics and unreal difficulties. We cannot discuss all this here. But it is certain even now that these criticisms do not seriously affect his work as a whole.

Since 1960 the signs of official recognition by the Church have become more and more apparent. In 1960, Karl Rahner was named consultor to the commission *De Sacramentis*, in preparation for the Second Vatican Council. In 1962, he accompanied Cardinal König of Vienna (a bishop who represents to a rare degree the ideal Pope John had in mind), as theological adviser, to the first session of the Council; there, too, he had the opportunity of explaining his ideas on the preparatory schemes before cardinals and bishops; finally he was chosen by Pope John to join the first group of 195 council experts and so was able to take part in the sessions of the Roman commissions during the first half of 1963. It may be possible at a later date to describe how highly Pope John spoke of Karl Rahner in 1962 in the garden at Castel Gandolfo.

On November 7 and 25, 1963, Rahner had private audiences with Pope Paul VI. The Pope thanked him for his work in theology and at the Council, telling him to continue boldly on the way he had opened; he also said that he had read several of his books and would like to keep in close contact with him. Rahner also attended the subsequent sessions of the Council.

On the occasion of his sixtieth birthday, March 5, 1964, he was given the honorary degree of doctor by the Catholic theological faculties of Münster and Strasbourg. This coincided with the publication of an enormous two-volume *Festschrift*, with contributions and congratulations from cardinals, bishops, theologians, philosophers and other scholars from all parts of the world.[36] Here, too, is further evidence of the importance of Karl Rahner's work for the Church and the world.

2 Basic Questions of Karl Rahner's Theology

The following attempts a brief survey of the theological positions taken up by Karl Rahner. Since this is the first time it has been done, I shall have to repeat—although from a different standpoint—some of what was said in the first part. But in this brief introduction I cannot hope to cover everything.

A preliminary remark may be permitted. Much of Rahner's work is simply an exposition of traditional teaching, particularly when it is a question of his lecture notes or of articles in a lexicon. To crave for originality at any price would be even less fitting in a Catholic theologian than in any other scholar. This is a fact, then, that need not be passed over with embarrassing silence. Here I want to try to show only where Rahner's independence and thus the progress of Catholic theology can be discerned. In all this it is not easy to find a simple and practical principle on which to base and arrange the material. Inevitably, perspectives partly overlap.

1. The philosophical fermentation of theology

Karl Rahner is convinced that we must *think* if we are to say anything that matters in theology. He is equally convinced that our thinking must begin from the modern situation, from *modern philosophy*; and that this may be done without preconceived ideas. He is finally convinced that the proper function of theology is not to look back and meditate on its history, but constantly to *renew the effort* of dealing with objective theological questions. Even when the development of dogma has led to the classical formulations of the Church's teaching authority, there remains more to do than simply repeat these classical formulations and explain historically how they came to be established. We may, therefore, understand some of Rahner's theological positions in the light of the basic positions of his philosophy.

We need not overrate the originality of this philosophy. It belongs to that group of essays in philosophy which even now can best be described by linking them with the name of Maréchal. This modern Christian philosophy cannot really any longer be called "neo-scholasticism", since—while holding this tradition in respect and even keeping it alive—it is in fact engaged in direct, unprejudiced and frank discussion with the philosophy of Kant, the German Idealists and contemporary Existentialism.[37] It is not merely the preservation of tradition.

Although they differ considerably among themselves, there is a unity of approach on the part of these philosophers, among whom may be mentioned Siewerth, Max Müller, Hayen, Marc, de Waelhens, Dondeyne, Welte, Lotz and Coreth. To describe their philosophy objectively, in very few words (and somewhat broadly), we might perhaps say this: it deliberately carries further a number of points raised by Aquinas, but understands modern philosophy from within and enters into discussion with it, while conceiving itself as a *transcendental philosophy*. That is to say: it unfolds the *a priori* conditions for the possibility of ontological knowledge and freedom in the subject itself. So it is able from its own resources to develop the themes of contemporary existentialist philosophy. It faces present-day philosophy; it is not merely anxious, on the defensive, but appreciates this "turning to the subject" (properly understood) as an event in the history of the mind, at root inspired by Christianity and its conception of man; so it belongs to the intellectual history of Christianity itself. Because of its anthropocentric, subjective (not "subjectivist") starting point, by contrast with the ancient cosmocentric outlook, this philosophy has an intimate understanding of man's history and of his historical condition. In such themes, embracing history and essence, it sees that a function of the philosophical situation is also imposed upon it ultimately by the Christian conception of existence.

Karl Rahner belongs to this group. His work on the epistemology of Aquinas, as I have already said, is meant to be fundamentally a systematic study and not merely the record of what others have thought in the past. If Rahner sees the human-finite spirit in its transcendental, *a priori* relationship to God, this is a conception which he owes to Maréchal's basic insight and he makes no secret of the fact. Rahner goes further by showing how human sensation emerges from the mind, how this mind can discover itself only by finding expression in symbols; he goes further by providing a transcendental foundation for man's turning to his concrete history—which cannot be explained in terms of any previous condition—as the real point at which the mind can discover its very self as that which is related to the mystery of the infinite.

In his second and last philosophical book, Rahner speaks of man as one who—in virtue of the synthesis of transcendence and history actually realized in him—is necessarily open to a revelation of God which can possibly enter into his history. Perhaps Rahner at that time, when writing *Hörer des Wortes*, did not see as clearly as he later stated it[38] that man's concrete nature, as he experiences it in history and presupposes—even if only implicitly—it in his philosophy, is already conditioned by a "supernatural existential". All of which means that, merely on the basis of a purely natural transcendentality, man can never in fact learn that he is open to a revelation which God may possibly grant; but he is also in his self-reflection already more than mere nature (even if, by simply reflecting on himself, he cannot distinguish what is his natural being and what is in fact an openness through grace to an actual, freely decided divine self-communication). All the same, Rahner's scheme of a philosophy of religion is distinguished from similar attempts in the Catholic field by the fact that he does not artificially construct a merely "natural religion". If this is done, it is all-too-easy to be content with the possession of such a "natural religion": thus a positive revealed religion would be imperilled, for it may then easily come too late to those who are satisfied with the "natural". When Rahner analyses the being to whom a possible revelation is addressed, he does not stick—like the average author of a work on fundamental theology—at a purely formal subject of objective knowledge. He does not establish the possibility of a revelation merely objectively, from the nature of God and his possible deeds. We can easily see what consequences this analysis may have for the preaching of positive revelation to modern man and to the modern world.

Do these basic philosophical views also have an effect on theology itself? For Karl Rahner they certainly have. The point must be raised here, since modern Christian philosophy on the whole has not yet had much influence on theology. In the history of dogma, the influence of the historical method is still too pronounced; systematic theology is often too much inclined to see possibilities of real progress only in peripheral questions and not in the decisive, basic positions of Christianity. Here I would like to point to just a few such influences of this modern philosophy on Rahner's theology.

First of all, there is his *theology of mystery*.[39] For Rahner, the fact that a truth is a mystery (a mystery, that is, of the Christian revelation), does not mean first and last a *negative* qualification of these truths, as if a mystery were always something *still* concealed from us, simply because we are human beings belonging to this world. It shows rather that the creaturely transcendence of the finite spirit is of its very nature related to mystery *as such*. Mystery alone is the true goal of knowing and loving transcendency, so that every quest for understanding arises from the abyss of mystery. And this mystery is man's beatitude. It is not dissolved in the intuitive vision of God, nor does it mean a mere limit to the beatific vision: it means rather that man *is* himself transcendency to mystery as such.

So, for Karl Rahner the three basic mysteries of Christianity—Trinity, Incarnation and Grace, which is completed in glory—are to be understood from this basic nature of man, without thereby losing their character as mystery and without the Incarnation and Grace ceasing to be free dispositions of God himself.

Incarnation and Grace are indeed *the two ways* in which absolute mystery freely and without any obligation communicates itself to man in absolute closeness. In them man's relationship to absolute mystery, the *potentia obedientialis*, is fulfilled.[40] There is here a real self-communication of God to the creature (Rahner defines it more closely as true "quasi-formal causality", as distinct from a created gift). Thus Rahner starts out from the word of revelation, from the "economic" relationship of God to the creature in the twofold "mission", and in this way reaches the necessary diversity in God of the two "processions" which are proper to God in himself. I do not think that any theologian has ever before approached this problem in the same way, namely, that the *divine trinity* in itself has something to do with God's treatment of man in history and vice versa. Rahner, using a theological "telegram style", formulates it thus: the economic trinity (God's triune nature for us) and the immanent trinity (God's triune nature in itself) are in reality the same.[41] But we have to be very cautious in using the concept of "person": it was easier for the theology of the early Church, not confronted as we are today with a notion of person which might lead us to a belief in three gods.

This is a philosophical theology, because Rahner understands man's transcendentality not only as a formal, purely neutral condition for his supernatural destiny and fulfilment, but as a preliminary draft in which these are implicitly contained, even though the order of the Incarnation and of Grace remains beyond all our deserts.

He makes further use of this basic conception to prepare the way for a deeper theological understanding of the mystery of the *hypostatic union* (the unity of God and man in Jesus Christ). It is an approach to be found today otherwise only in the work of B. Welte and F. Malmberg.[42] On this topic also only a brief comment is possible here.

Rahner sees man's nature in its transcendentality in such a way that the hypostatic union—obviously freely chosen by God and in no way due to us—is conceived as the supreme actualization of what man is as spirit. Thus the opposition between a merely static, ontic Christology and a modernistic consciousness-Christology is overcome in a truly ontological Christology.

In this context, Rahner wrestles particularly with the problem of how Jesus is not a God dealing with us in human form, but really God and simultaneously truly man, so that both dogmatic theology and exegesis (with the data obtained from "the quest of the historical Jesus") can therefore be right. To solve the problem, he starts out from the fact that only a *divine* person can possess a freedom really distinct from him as his own, in such wise that it does not cease to be truly free even in regard to the divine person who possesses it and yet qualifies this person himself as its ontological subject. "For we can conceive of no one but God personally constituting a being distinct from himself."[43] From this standpoint, incidentally, we can maintain the Catholic teaching that the human consciousness of Jesus has an immediacy to the divine essence (that is, his human soul had even on earth the *visio immediata*, the intuitive vision of God) and yet respect the biblical accounts of his "learning", "not knowing"—in a word, of his growth as a man.

This philosophy of the transcendentality of the human mind provides Rahner with an opportunity of solving the old controversy between thomists and molinists.[44] Even if the reader is not trained in theology, it is to be hoped that he will read on at this point: for we are concerned with one of Rahner's central themes, from which magnificent prospects emerge.

In the theology of the schools the controversy centres on the question whether a salutary act (a human act raised to a higher mode of being by the supernatural grace of God) needs a proper "formal object", which cannot be attained by a purely natural act.

Here Rahner brings a new factor into the discussion: a *transcendental experience* which cannot be formulated as theme, concept or proposition, in which the formal object is present not in the manner of an object but as an unspecified horizon—and yet is truly present. Thus Rahner strictly maintains—against Molina and against a good many of the post-Tridentine theologians—the thomist doctrine of a proper formal object for every supernatural, salutary act. But he does not stop at the difficulty usually raised against this doctrine : man "perceives" nothing of such a formal object. For according to Rahner the unspecified, *a priori* openness of the natural mind towards being as such and the unspecified *a priori* transcendentality of the mind elevated by supernatural grace are (from the nature of the case) so interlocked with one another that a secondary reflexion cannot necessarily draw one away from the other. And even without direct reflexion, the dynamism directed towards the absolute self-communication of God can therefore be really present in consciousness and have an effect on man's individual and collective mental history. And in this respect we cannot necessarily distinguish it from the unlimited, natural transcendental openness of man.

These considerations lead Rahner to the idea of a *universal and yet supernatural revelation* which is of great importance for the interpretation of redemptive history and of the relationship of Christianity to non-Christians and to non-Christian religions.[45] Rahner takes as his basis the fundamental principles of Catholic theology, the import of which has not yet been measured : God wills the salvation of all men, even though they are in a fallen state. This supernatural will for salvation means for all men at all times—because of Jesus Christ— the offer of supernatural grace (as an interior, really existing factor in the individual and collective history of the human mind), no matter whether this grace is accepted or rejected. These are principles which bind every Catholic theologian.

Rahner argues : Such a communication of grace then means also a change in man's transcendental mental horizon, within which he carries on his history. And there exists also from the very beginning something like a universal history of a transcendental character concerned with a revelation which reaches *all men*. But that is not to say that man is at all times, at every spatial-temporal point of his history, in an objective dialogue with God, formulated and given expression in propositions: in this sense there is not everywhere and at all times an express, thematic, special and official history of revelation. Such a history exists only when God speaks to man also in human words, which can be given conceptual expression, and confirms by signs and wonders the legitimacy of this incarnation of the absolute, divine word in the human. But because of the universality of God's will to save and because of the supernatural grace of Christ in all men, there is nevertheless everywhere already a universal history of revelation: for every free self-communication of God to man may be called revelation, even if it occurs first of all in the transcendental and not yet in the categorial region of human consciousness.

Here lies the pointer to Rahner's doctrine of the "anonymous Christian" and of the "believer in God and Jesus Christ", who in fact thinks that he does not or cannot believe. If what has been said is correct, then there must and can be human beings who have a transcendental, supernatural experience and who by reason of their freedom have accepted this in faith and charity, but who misinterpret it in conceptual terms. That is why such people maintain—in what is always a secondary reflexion—that they are not Christians, perhaps even that they are not theists.

From this starting point we can also recognize in *non-Christian religions* at the historical stage before their real confrontation with Christianity the character of a legitimate religion (in the theological sense, not merely in the sense of a self-evident social toleration).[46] According to the Catholic notion of religion, man can live and necessarily lives only in a religion that is organized socially: it follows that every religion—socially and historically established—that we really meet in a person's historical environment and is, within that environment, the "better", must have in the divine intention of salvation a positive salutary function for that person, and must be "legitimate" for him.

As we see from the Old Testament example, it is not absolutely necessary to the notion of a legitimate religion that in its concrete-historical form there are present only elements positively willed by God. It is not absolutely necessary that an adequate and institutionally established criterion exist to distinguish between divinely willed factors and the phenomena of human degeneration in this religion. It is not absolutely necessary that conceptual reflexion on the religious person's supernatural, transcendental, basic experience of God's grace-giving closeness should always be successful (even if it is never completely lacking and will never be entirely unsuccessful). Finally, it is not absolutely necessary for this historically progressing conceptual reflexion on the basic mystery of religion to be expressed in a form which can be grasped historically and reflexively as given and legitimized by God—as it is in the eschatological situation of Christianity, in which the God-man is present and grasped by faith as the absolute and final synthesis of divine self-giving and its human acceptance.

The metaphysics of the transcendentality of the finite mind—of which we are still speaking here—is applied by Rahner, surprisingly enough, to the doctrine of creation.[47] In this respect he develops and deepens the transcendental philosophy of Maréchal. Absolute being is seen not merely as the goal—static in itself—of the spirit, towards which the latter would move in virtue of

61

its own dynamism, but as the moving force of this movement itself. The doctrine of final causes begins again to be taken seriously. Absolute being is the inner force of the spirit's self-movement, without thereby becoming a constitutive element of the being of the finite spirit itself.

Rahner then takes this relation of the absolute spirit to finite being as an instance or example of the becoming of any being at all: there is a becoming of a created being when that becoming arises from the creature's active potency; in principle, this is *self-transcendence*, in which this being actively seeking fulfilment surpasses itself in virtue of that absolute being which inwardly belongs to it, without thereby constituting a part of its nature. From this conclusion Rahner attempts a synthesis between the teaching of faith on the one hand—namely, that all finite being is created and that there are essential differences between the individual spheres of being—and on the other the conception of the world as an evolutionary, ascending process. If it could thus be shown that the notion of active self-transcendence in virtue of absolute being is irreducibly original and legitimate, that would be very important for the future. The traditional theological notions of the divine conservation of the world and God's concurrence with creatures could be grasped in a modern and deeper fashion; at the same time, the world in all its structures would be left to its own laws (the "secular world"), without this necessarily involving a profanation.

Finally, the doctrine of the transcendentality of the finite spirit provides also the background for Karl Rahner's efforts—which, of course, he shares with other important theologians of the present time—to establish the true difference between nature and grace in such a way as to avoid any "extrinsicism" in the theology of grace. "Nature" cannot and must not be conceived as in the concrete complete in itself, rounded off and obvious, with grace as something granted over and above all this as an unsought and unnecessary gift: rather in the same way that a house with a perfectly habitable first storey might unexpectedly have a second artificially placed above it.[48]

2. *Theology called to preaching*

I would like to emphasize once again what I said already in the first part of this little book: we would misunderstand the work of Karl Rahner if we were to regard his theories as primarily inspired by speculative-philosophical interests. The impulses coming from the present-day state of spiritual distress (which is concealed by our technical, positivist outlook), that is, from pastoral concern—in other words, the kerygmatic and pastoral-theological inspiration—are in principle more decisive for him personally and for his work. Naturally, it is not possible to trace back easily and clearly Rahner's quite definite particular theories, but this inspiration does really penetrate his whole theology. No matter how greatly he appreciates the value of theological-historical work, he refuses for his own part even more decisively to be a scientific theologian for the sake of theological scholarship. We must therefore mention in this context also his less scholarly enterprises: books of sermons, of prayer and devotion, and reviews of gramophone records —all of which might easily ruin a scholar's reputation in Germany. Nor is the composition of a theological pocket dictionary the way to harvest the laurels of scholarship.

As with the plans I mentioned earlier, all this can be understood in one way only: by every means and as well as he possibly can, he seeks to help the priest and the educated layman to preach afresh and to seize in its original spirit the old Gospel, so that it really reaches man in his present situation. To Rahner it does not really matter at all whether or not such an enterprise appears scholarly. The same mentality can be seen also in the thick volume of collected essays on pastoral theology, with its acute analyses of the situation of the Church and of Christianity today and with its bold programme for the Church's future.[49] Whether he is talking there about pastoral care of prisoners, parish libraries, our attitude to modern literature, missions in the railway-stations or anything else, he is determined to bring together reflections on theological principles and the practice of a Christian life.

Two aspects, which are characteristic of this attitude, deserve special mention. First, there is an emphasis on the spiritual and social *pluralism* of the modern world, and the diaspora situation of the Church and the individual Christian which results from this. Rahner explains that this is a redemptive-historical "must" for the Christian to view and appreciate without prejudice. He is always insisting that the Christian and the Church today can exist only if they cease to be anxious and on the defensive in a Christian and ecclesiastical ghetto (mental, cultural and ecclesiastico-political); if they are able to appreciate the worldliness of the world as something which from the standpoint of Christianity must be something positively willed by God. That is not to render innocuous this world, its guilt and its peril.

The worldliness of the world corresponds in principle to the Christian belief in its pure createdness and in the essential difference between nature and grace: it springs from this faith. It is therefore a Christian duty and virtue to endure the persistent and—once again—plural worldliness of the world in patience and sober realism precisely in its earthly structures, not wanting to bring about by force the kingdom of God either in an ecclesiastical state or in a direct consecration of the earthly spheres: for the Church is still only a beginning, a promise and a sacrament of the kingdom of God. If the worldliness of the world is seen as completely legitimate, if it is recognized that its persistent opposition to the Gospel has to the very end a redemptive-historical function, inevitably serving the salvation and grace of Christ even in an "anonymous Christianity", then the prognoses of "Christianity's chances" may be sober and yet hopeful.[50] The Christian can be a confessor of the Gospel, a witness to Christ, without slipping into the rôle of a narrow-minded sectarian and monomanic ideologist, without making God's power and God's mercy cease at the point where he himself or his Church reaches a frontier.

Secondly, the *ecumenical motive* is essential in Karl Rahner's theology. A theological attitude which recognizes the pluralism of the contemporary world partly as a necessity springing from the nature of man, partly as a redemptive-historical "must", cannot overlook the fact of Christian divisions. It cannot ignore the fact that Catholic theology can also learn from Evangelical, and not merely in matters of history and exegesis. Thus we can always perceive in Rahner's work an effort to learn from Evangelical theology, using its presentation of problems to extend the horizon of his own questioning, and—without falling into a false irenicism—so to formulate his own theology and the Church's dogma that these present to Evangelical Christians and theologians only those difficulties in understanding which simply cannot be avoided. Only from this standpoint can a good deal of what Rahner has said on "the many Masses and the one sacrifice", on "transubstantiation", indulgences, the notion of *opus operatum*, and the personal aspect of the efficacy of the sacraments, be quite justly appreciated.[51]

In all this there constantly appears one of Rahner's fundamental preoccupations: even a dogmatically binding and permanently valid formulation must not be regarded as the final stage—never to be surpassed—of a development now brought to its close. It must be seen also as a formulation which—without prejudice to its permanent validity—is open on to the mystery, which never says everything that is true and important from the Christian standpoint, which can create for non-Catholics real difficulties in understanding and therefore likewise constantly imposes on Catholic theology a task to be fulfilled anew. What Rahner had been saying and trying to do for years was confirmed at the highest level by Pope John XXIII in his cheering words at the first session of the Council—a test of the loyalty to the Church of those representatives of a nervous intolerance who otherwise appealed on all occasions to the Pope. Rahner's work is inspired by the thought that the Catholic theologian must always look for the "guilt", for what causes the opposition of other Christians to the theology of his Church, in himself also: for his Catholic theology, too, remains a *theologia viatoris et peccatoris*, a theology of the pilgrim and the sinner.

3. *The diversity and multiplicity of theological problems*

What has to be said in this third section may at first sight create the impression that I have gathered together here simply what I could not bring under the first two headings: in other words, that it is not really a genuine aspect of Karl Rahner's theology. But it is different if we look at the matter more closely. Characteristic of Karl Rahner is the way he adapts himself to the variety of problems brought to him. I want to try to analyse the temporal-historical reason for this.

The period after the first world war meant for the life of the Church and also—involved in this—for theology a definite break and to some extent a new beginning, sharply distinguished from the Church's earlier conservative and defensive attitude. We may recall the movement for liturgical revival, the fact that Catholics were at least in part familiar with the forms of the democratic State (as, for instance, freedom of the press) and undertook political responsibility within the really modern States where Church and politics were kept completely apart. We may recall what was said in the first section about the transformation of philosophy from an essentially restorative neo-scholasticism to a Christian philosophy which is obviously a part of modern intellectual life; we may also mention the emergence of a Catholic literature which no longer confuses comfortable bourgeois sentiment with literary power. We may mention a new Christian art which is no longer neo-gothic, Nazarene or a youthful style; we can look at the new appreciation of the independence, literacy and world-responsibility of the laity, no longer merely objects of the clergy's spiritual ministrations, but active holders of human and Christian functions—and that indeed in the Church's sphere.

When we reflect on this transformation, we can say today in retrospect that the *first generation*, which attained the peak of its social, intellectual and ecclesiastical achievement between the two world wars, brought this new mentality only in a very general way into theology. It was still too early for the new spirit to have an effect on the handling of technical theological problems. In Germany, for instance, theologians like Peter Lippert, Romano Guardini, Erich Przywara and others opened the new period of theology still more or less in a general fashion. They represented the new spirit, but they scarcely entered into the really individual theological problems.

The theological text-books, therefore, which certainly go into details, took no notice of these great representatives of the new period. Their names are not to be found in the text-books at all. But there are other reasons for this.

The new movements in the Church arose—and indeed partly arise today—not properly within theology and Christian philosophy at their scientific level. They arose rather out of the life of the Church herself, not from the "official" and, therefore, far too readily conservative circles, but from those which are interested from both the religious and intellectual points of view. The new beginnings in theology, therefore, were seen at first and almost inevitably in the literary form known as *haute vulgarisation*. We must not be too quick to seize on the unpleasant after-taste this word has. We must not think that there can be no genuine and creative achievement in this form of literature. But we can also understand that the themes have to be very general in order to be sure of an immediate interest on the part of this class of reader. Guardini's, Lippert's or even Karl Adam's works are typical in this respect.

Finally, there is one thing that we must not forget. This first generation between the two world wars had experienced the trauma of modernism in their youth when they were studying philosophy and theology and had known that reaction of the Church—perhaps on the whole necessary—which in the intrigues and heresy-hunting of integralism betrayed its all-too-human and indeed repulsive side.[52] It is not surprising that this generation often anxiously avoided tackling or dealing systematically with themes which, they feared, were bound to give rise to conflicts. The tendency at the time was to side-step these dangers from the beginning by choosing both theme and style in such a way that they were without interest to "informers" and "denouncers".

One exegete wrote biblical novels, another plunged into a harmless history of the Vulgate, the third changed sides from exegesis to moral theology—a safe subject at the time. If the dogmatic theologian had no desire or gift for discussion with educated people in the Church or despisers of religion outside her, he simply concentrated on editing texts, the retrospective history of dogma, and left the official theology of the schools as it had hitherto been. This may be seen in the manuals—thorough in their way and respectable—of Bartmann, Diekamp, Pohle, Van Noort and Tanquerey. It was possible in those years to become famous by editing a few medieval manuscripts; in that way, one became sure of a mention later in the theological dictionaries. But one question was never raised: had the earlier theology been so stupid as not to observe what "treasures" were reposing in these manuscripts? or did much remain unprinted two or three hundred years ago because it was not worth printing?

It is from these positions alone that the peculiar character of the *second generation* can be understood. It can no longer be content with proclaiming a new spirit, an open attitude, unprejudiced towards the modern age, its mentality and art. It can no longer be satisfied with the fact that the new spirit exercises an influence solely on the practice of the Christian life. It must face the whole range of individual problems in philosophy, theology and the life of the Church, and here vindicate the new spirit—it must show that this belongs both to the Church and to the present time, not only in general but in the immeasurable complexity of individual problems. Only when this really succeeds, can Christians feel—so far as that is possible in a world of sorrows—the present as an obvious sphere of existence, completely in accordance with Christianity. Only then does it become clear that we have to do more than defend Christianity against

69

a new age: we have to present Christianity as the new, divine response—which today alone is really complete and intelligible—to the question which our historical present and the future advancing upon it impose and are. It cannot be said that the second generation in general is devoting itself to this task with particularly great zeal and success. But there are advantages in this: all the patriotic and nationalist tones are finally vanishing from theology, for this second generation is forced into international co-operation. All the same, we gain the impression that the tempo of the present time provides more tasks than can really be mastered by the theologians.

It is only by reflecting on what has just been said that we can properly understand the unique character of Rahner's theology. We shall see that what I want to say in this third section, in spite of the disparity and diversity of the themes, can nevertheless be appreciated from a unified standpoint. In face of the "diversity and multiplicity" of the problems, I have attempted neither a systematic nor an exhaustive treatment, but sought merely to indicate how a theologian of the second generation attempts for his part to do justice to the tasks outlined here. But the reader must keep in mind both these horizons within which all Rahner's individual works must be considered. Rahner's basic attitude is—by contrast with the ancient cosmocentrism—anthropocentric (and thereby radically theocentric and christocentric); it is transcendental and personalist, it takes man's historicity and his "existence" seriously. And all this theology is intended to serve a kerygmatic function, so that the harmony of Christianity with the mentality of the present time can come into the open.

I begin then with the problem of the *development of*

dogma.[53] In spite of all the difficulties arising from the history of dogma, Rahner insists that we can understand this development rightly and from the Catholic standpoint only if we stick to the principle that the understanding of faith in the Apostolic Church and in the Church today are closely linked with one another even on the conceptual plane and in logical reflexion. The unfolding of dogma cannot be left *merely* to an irrational instinct of faith, beyond rational explanation, or to the *formal* authority of the Church's teaching office *alone*. Naturally, the history of dogma is largely a history of the way in which what had been present implicitly became explicit. Obviously, this implication involves a mental reality in which the elements are not merely concepts. Obviously also, the process of making explicit takes place primarily in the Church's historically developing understanding of faith and not merely in the theologian's study. But Rahner emphatically declares that this process of making explicit must in principle—at least after the event—be capable of being worked out logically (although this does not mean that the certainty of the conclusion rests solely upon the stringency of such a logical-conceptual elaboration). If this were not so, says Rahner, the development of dogma would no longer preserve the revelation which closed with the apostolic preaching, but would be imperceptibly transformed into a new post-apostolic revelation. This campaign for a correctly understood rationality in theology has various consequences.

More clearly than some theologians in fact see it, Rahner explains first of all that if theologians in their work rightly appeal to the Church's understanding of the faith today and to the decisions of the teaching authority today, they can indeed in this way reach a legitimate conclusion of faith. But they are not thereby released from the duty of showing *how* the modern dogma was contained in the apostolic preaching or how it can be proved by a legitimate logical process of being made explicit as really revealed by God himself. When we recall this, we can at once understand the position which Karl Rahner adopts—with many other theologians in the wake of J. R. Geiselmann—in regard to the relation between *Tradition and Scripture*[54] and which he vehemently defended at the second Vatican Council.

If we place the above-mentioned demand before tradition and theology, and consider soberly and objectively how much (or, better, how little) we know historically of this tradition, then a theologian can no longer claim that ancient tradition offers us more by way of really binding, material contents of faith than is also contained in Scripture—apart perhaps from the single instance of our knowledge through faith of the delimitation of the canon of Scripture. At least for us, tradition cannot in practice and in the concrete be placed alongside Scripture as a materially distinct source of the contents of faith: it is, on the contrary, the formal authority which carries Scripture, declares it to be sacred Scripture, that is to say, determines its canon. This means that we must not conceive the authentication of the canon by tradition alone as one example *among others* of how tradition mediates a truth of faith which is found neither explicitly nor implicitly in Scripture. If then we conceive the Tridentine statement on the relation between Scripture and Tradition in this way, we could also come to an understanding with Protestant theology on this problem: for Protestant theology also has gradually learned that Scripture itself is carried by the apostolic oral kerygma of Christ's authorized messengers, that it is the solid substance of this teaching, remains constantly dependent upon it, and can never be understood otherwise than as an instrument of the authoritatively teaching Church (no matter how much this Church precisely in this respect places herself under the word of God in Scripture, interprets this and adds nothing "new" to it).

If we adopt this doctrine, that Scripture is in practice materially sufficient for us, without in any way questioning the importance of the teaching office and of tradition, then we must also have a well thought out idea of the ways in which the later Church can render explicit the apostolic kerygma. And Karl Rahner has a very exact idea of this. He does not restrict these possibilities of the later Church by the sceptical positivism of the exegetes who are no more than that or of the pure historians—of those who, unless their own spirit moves them, make the ancient letter so rigid that its content can no longer be unfolded in history. In a lengthy manuscript already completed before the definition of the bodily assumption of Mary into heaven, Rahner demonstrated his theory of the development of dogma precisely with reference to this most extreme case. He shows there how Mary's assumption into heaven is really contained materially in Scripture and bases the "new" dogma on divine revelation. How ironical that a small mind was able from 1950 onwards to hold up the publication precisely of this work which might have spared the Church so many malicious attacks!

Karl Rahner's doctrine of the *Inspiration of Scripture* also has sometimes been grotesquely misunderstood. It has been asserted that he taught a "collective inspiration".[55] There can be no question of this; but one may well be surprised to see how incapable some theologians are of reading their colleagues' books (and what simplicity of mind is betrayed in book reviews). For Rahner also, it is the actual author of the individual book who is inspired by God and no one else. But, he maintains,

this divine inspiration of the individual biblical author
takes place directly and formally in order that this work
of his should emerge *as* a factor in making the apostolic
kerygma objective and as a book of the "primitive
Church", believing on account of this apostolic kerygma.

The purpose of inspiration is, therefore, first of all, to
ensure that by means of it this primitive Church (because
of the apostolic witness) should become and should be
the permanent and irrevocable norm of faith for the
later Church: it can become and be such by thus being
made objective. From this standpoint it is easy for
Rahner to understand why the determination of the
canon could have a long history: his problem is to establish how the Church's authoritative understanding of the
canon may be legitimized. For this purpose, there is no
need to appeal—as used to be done—to explicit apostolic
testimony to the inspiration of each particular book.
Such testimony is neither obvious nor historically
plausible. Nor do we need to postulate new, later revela-
tions—which in fact would not be compatible with the
Church's teaching that apostolic revelation is closed.
Without any new revelation, by reason of her living
awareness of faith, the later Church can distinguish the
legitimate objectification of the apostolic Church's awareness of faith from other religious testimonies of the first
age—and it does not matter when she does this. If we
assume that God formally set up the primitive Church's
understanding of faith as the enduring norm for the later
belief of the Church precisely through the fact of the
emergence of the New Testament Scriptures and their
becoming through inspiration the word of God in the
proper sense of that term, then the determination—possible without new revelation—of how to objectify the
faith of the primitive Church by the later Church is of
itself and simultaneously also the determination of

the canon of the Scriptures, which are the word of God himself.

From the *ecclesiology* of Karl Rahner I shall select here only the more important themes. Rahner attempts to define more precisely the relationship between the *papal primacy and the episcopate.*[56] He wants to render intelligible the doctrine that the bishops—in spite of the pope's universal primacy of jurisdiction, even over the bishops—are not the pope's subalterns, but (in the biblical sense) "pasture" their "flock" in the name of Christ himself and always form together the supreme ruling body in the Church, which itself possesses supreme authority in teaching and legislating in union with the pope but not properly as derived from him (for this would be a contradiction of the very idea of supreme authority).

Rahner insists that while the episcopal college can *never* be conceived as independent of the pope or as an institution with its own competence set up over against him, the pope always and everywhere acts *as* the competent head of the episcopal college. Personal primacy of jurisdiction and primacy in teaching belong to the pope because he is personal head of the episcopal college, which acts in him and through him even when he is acting alone. This is clear from the fact that there exists the above-mentioned teaching of faith on the bishops and that the pope is not tied to definite and immutable legal formalities in regard to the rest of the episcopate in order to be able to act as head and representative of the college. If it were maintained that there existed such definite formalities, legal and legally controllable, binding the pope once and for all, then pope and episcopal college would be two distinct juridical subjects, and at any particular time the line of demarcation between their powers would have to be legally determined. But this is just what

cannot be done. The pope is not subject to any im
mutable, legally controllable principles in regard to his
concrete relationship to the rest of the episcopate. But he
acts always *as* head of the supreme governing body in
the Church, which has over itself no higher authority:
for that of the pope is certainly higher than that of any
individual bishop, but he acts *precisely with* the authority of the personal head of the whole episcopate. The
result is that papal rule over the whole Church has always
to be finding new ways—historically conditioned as these
must be—of maintaining its connection with the universal
episcopate, which is never merely a body of men who
obediently receive papal instructions, but remains—
together with the pope—that supreme holder of authority
in the Church which is under the Spirit of God alone.
There is no doubt that this doctrine of Rahner's has
already had its effect on the form and statements of the
Council.

In a further question handled by the Council, it seems
as if Rahner has had to revise his attitude. Many years
ago he was at pains to study obediently and objectively
the encyclical, *Mystici Corporis*, and to justify its teaching on *membership of the Church*.[57] By contrast with this
encyclical, under the distinguished leadership of Cardinal
Bea, the tendency today is to attribute Church-member-
ship to every baptized person, non-Roman Catholics also.
But Rahner's interpretation still has permanent value:
he shows that this question always involves a positive-
legal decision on terminology. The Church can prescribe
a terminology without thereby settling the matter itself,
and thus another future variation in terminology is not
excluded. Obviously this opens up tremendous prospects,
particularly when the Church enters into a dialogue also
with non-Christians. Incidentally, Rahner tries in a
variety of ways[58] to help the person in the Church who

has to admit that the Church is causing him unavoidable suffering and grave disappointment.

Rahner's study of the *Church and the sacraments*[59] brings out new aspects by comparison with the traditional sacramental theology. He understands a sacrament as an act of the Church's total self-realization in regard to the individual human being. The sacraments are thus not merely means of grace in the hands of the Church, but events in which the Church actualizes her own nature. The concept, *opus operatum*, is rendered intelligible from the nature of the Church: there is an *opus operatum* only in the time of the Church considered as eschatological time, in which divine grace is both victorious and tangible; it is not dependent on a purely legal disposition of God. In this way also he is able to show how the seven sacraments of the Catholic Church can be conceived as "instituted" by Jesus Christ himself even if Christ's express words of institution are not preserved for every sacrament—indeed, even if such an express foundation is unlikely. With a deliberate ecumenical aim, Rahner develops a theory of the connection between *word and sacrament* in the Church.[60] The sacramental word, he says, is altogether the most intensive and the perfect example of the effective word in the Church. Thus word and sacrament are not ultimately opposed to one another: the word, too, is the realization of the Church as she is also realized and revealed in the sacraments.

In his little book, *The Many Masses and the One Sacrifice*,[61] Rahner took up a question which is of considerable importance for both ecumenical discussion and the Church's practice. The question is, how often the sacrifice of the Mass ought to be offered, and whether there is a handy norm to decide this which would satisfy both the real dogmatic principles and practical needs. In this connexion, Rahner has never questioned—as has been asserted—or even obscured the fact that every Mass is an act of Christ himself as high priest, since it is willed because of Christ's command to commemorate him, and therefore every Mass takes place in the name of Christ. But, he says, we cannot draw from this a principle to decide how often Mass ought to be celebrated. For the number of Masses does not increase the act of the one earthly and heavenly Christ who carries them all.

Every Mass as an act of Christ has infinite value, but many Masses do not increase the one act of Christ and the honour of God arising out of this in so far as it is realized *precisely* by Christ. Rahner strongly emphasizes that the Mass as a new and multipliable sacrifice is a sacrifice within the dimensions of a cultic sign (sacrament as distinct from *res sacramenti*), but not within the dimensions of reality signified and made present by the Mass—that is, within the dimensions of the unique sacrifice of Christ on the cross. He then brings in the doctrine that formal reverence to God is possible only through genuine moral acts as such (being acts of Christ or of the members of the Church). From all this he argues: the Mass means an increase of honour to God and a growth in grace for those who take part in it, as far and as often as in the Mass and through the grace bestowed in it *ex opere operato* a greater existential, believing and loving participation of those at Mass (priest and people) is practically possible. If this is not to be expected, a further increase in Masses has no meaning. There may then be circumstances in which it is just as good or better for a priest to take part with devotion in another's Mass than to celebrate himself (whether we can speak of concelebration in this connexion, is another question).[62] This conclusion is very important for all those places where Mass is sometimes said hastily, in the midst of disturbing factors, or in one church simultaneously at many altars—as, for example, in monasteries, at congresses, at pilgrimage centres and during retreats.

These considerations also form the basis of Rahner's pastoral-theological reflexions on the *sacrifice of the Mass and an ascesis for youth*.[63] The liturgy must always take such a form that the *opus operatum* is not confused with a magical event. For *opus operatum* never implies a mechanical, impersonal effect, but the absolutely assured divine word of forgiveness: and sanctification becomes effective only to the extent in which it is accepted in a truly existential participation. Therefore, this effective word of God in the liturgy must be so spoken that it is able to call forth this existential realization in the most intensive way possible. This is what must be considered first of all in any reform of the liturgy: not respect for historical, non-divine traditions.

Karl Rahner was one of the first professional theologians to assert forthrightly the need for a genuine *renewal of the diaconate*,[64] even though he deliberately avoids over-estimating the importance of the sacramental and institutional aspects in the Church. He argues in this way: in the Church today there exist in fact those offices which were exercised in the early Church by deacons; and there is no reason why these (mostly married) men should be refused that confirmation and sacramental consecration which has always existed and still exists in the Church, but which today is given to those who have no need at all of it, those who will shortly afterwards be ordained priests. When we produced together *Diaconia in Christo*, we were not concerned merely with suggesting to the Church's official leaders ways in which aid could be provided for the most urgent pastoral needs (that deacons might visit the sick, bring them Holy Communion, take burial services, bless marriages—quite apart from baptizing, preaching and taking services in the absence of the priest, which always belonged to the deacon's office), but also to give a renewed emphasis to the fact that the office of ruling and of sacramental order in the Church are a service. "Your brothers, who serve you as pastors," was the title adopted by the bishops at the beginning of the Council in 1962. Moreover, the existence of married deacons would be a token of appreciation of the Eastern Churches' tradition—and, indeed, of the sacrament of matrimony.

In many studies and articles, Rahner has tried to revive again in the consciousness of the faithful some "forgotten truths" on the *sacrament of Penance*.[65] For this there must be a deeper reflexion on the Scriptural texts about guilt and its forgiveness; but there is also needed a new insight into the nature of "contrition", which "hurts", not because an individual deed is supposed to hurt at the moment, but because the sinner has to break down the system of values he has set up. It must be remembered, above all, that every sin is also a sin against the Church: that "auricular confession" is not a Catholic invention, but a relaxation of the severe penitential practice of the early Church; the sacrament of Penance today, just as in the early Church, shows the sinner placed at a distance, then received again into full communion when the sacrament is realized. Rahner emphasizes the fact that absolution is the assurance of peace with the Church, granted by the Church herself, and that this peace with the Church is the *res et sacramentum* of the reconciliation with God; that the acts of the penitent are an inner, constitutive factor of the penitential liturgy, by which the sinner places himself before the judgment of God's grace, and accepts contritely the divine forgiveness.

In his *theology of priestly existence*,[66] Rahner is concerned with the unity of the cultic and the prophetic elements in the priestly life. The priest sets out from the altar; the primal word that he speaks is the sacramental word, but precisely in virtue of his being empowered to utter that word he has the commission in season or out of season to preach the word of God wherever he is sent by the Church, as commissioned from above, not by reason of his situation in the world (as the layman is commissioned).

In order now to close the account of Rahner's theology of the Church, I would like also to refer to his assertion that the *bishop* has not only a genuinely official mission in regard to his own diocese, but a commission and a responsibility also in regard to the universal Church: for he can rightly be bishop of his particular Church only in so far as he is in addition, by logical priority, a member of the universal episcopate, of the one governing body of the universal Church under and with the pope.[67] The bishop counts as successor of the apostles, not because he is the successor of an individual apostle (which really would be difficult to prove), but because he belongs to the universal episcopate: this as a college is successor to the college of the apostles. Naturally, the bishop's membership of this governing body is realized in the concrete through the pope: this is recognized by the fact that the pope assigns to the bishop a definite territory.

It would be easier to write a book about Rahner's *theology of grace* than to explain it in a few lines to a reader who is not familiar with the text-book theology and therefore cannot very easily observe the differences in Rahner's treatment of the subject.

First of all, we must mention his doctrine of *uncreated grace*. Rahner seeks neither to deny nor obscure the factor of created grace as the effect of uncreated grace.

But for him grace is first and foremost uncreated grace, that is, the self-communication of God. "God's self-communication" is perhaps the central idea of Rahner's theology. In explaining it, he seizes on a word coined by medieval theology in an attempt to explain the beatific vision: quasi-formal causality. For Rahner, God's self-communication means that God by a quasi-formal causality communicates his own reality to the spiritual creature, and gives this to the creature as its own. The word, "quasi-formal causality", serves to distinguish this from the creation of a reality distinct from God out of nothing. Thus the nature of the entire supernatural order of grace is based on this quasi-formal causality. Every creation of a finite being belongs "in itself" to the natural order. God's self-communication is grace absolutely speaking—obviously it has also "created" consequences in the subject to which God communicates himself.[68]

There are, accordingly, two such self-communications of God: that involved in the very fact of God's becoming man and that of grace, which is fulfilled in final glory. A simple philosophical reflexion suffices to show that this is grace absolutely speaking. Since to every finite being there can be attributed connatural knowledge, namely, the "being-with-itself" of this finite being to the extent of its possession of being, a finite being as such cannot be a mystery properly so-called—but the basic truths of Christianity *are* mysteries. But vice versa, the basic mysteries of Christianity are not arbitrarily chosen (and must not be preached as if they were the result of arbitrary decrees); they have their reason in these two divine self-communications, which are mysteries because they are rooted in God's own incomprehensibility: the reason for both self-communications—as I said already in another connexion in the first part of this book—lies in the immanent Trinity of God, based on the two inner-divine "processions".

At this stage, Rahner introduces a further sequence of thought. Creation is God's free act: God could have created a world in which such a divine self-communication to his creature would not have taken place. And yet the possibility of creating out of nothing is for God ultimately an inner factor of his higher and more comprehensive possibility of expending himself ecstatically on what is not God.[69] Thus Rahner renders intelligible the inner unity of nature and grace (together with and in spite of the ontological differences between them, constituting nature as something "other" which grace itself presupposes as the condition of its possibility), the unity of the theology of grace and Christology, and the possibility of a Christocentrism which embraces the orders of creation and grace.

In the first section of this second part, it was already pointed out that Rahner differs from the usual tradition of the Jesuit school in teaching quite definitely that the "entitative" elevation through grace of the salutary act necessarily involves a supernatural formal object for every such act. In his transcendental philosophy, being and being-with-itself are the same thing: a being, therefore, returns into itself to the extent that it is being and is not itself alienated from being through the real non-being of matter. From which it follows that the supreme existential reality of the conscious spirit—grace—cannot be pure ontic reality beyond the reach of consciousness, but must have an ontological status: this also is in accordance with the teaching of Scripture and Tradition that grace is illumination and inspiration. Grace is therefore also essentially always *experience of grace*.[70] This does not mean that the conscious reality of grace is something appearing within the horizon of consciousness and at that

83

point a proper, definable, objective reality. Consciousness of grace means rather an alteration of man's transcendental horizon itself, which cannot in any way be unambiguously objectified and defined through immediate reflexion. But this does not mean that such an experience of grace is a contradiction of the notion of faith: faith is precisely the acceptance of such a direct self-communication of God and his self-revelation in itself and (where this exists) in its conceptual expression in human words guaranteed by official revelation. I might point out once again how important this teaching is for an "anonymous Christianity" and for a just Christian appreciation of non-Christian religions.

The first Catholic scientific-theoretical reflexions on the meaning of theological anthropology were those of Rahner in the first volume of the *Lexikon für Theologie und Kirche* under the heading, "Anthropology"; in Volume VII of this lexicon he drafted a brief sketch of such a doctrine of man under the title "Man". I cannot and will not simply repeat here these summary presentations. But I may be permitted to draw attention to four special themes of his dogmatic anthropology.

If Rahner—to the surprise of some contemporary professional theologians and informed laymen—has frequently been occupied with the question of devotion to the Sacred Heart, this was not merely in order to give greater depth to a devotion which had been especially fostered in the Society of Jesus, but also with a view to the horizons of his theology. If he analyses more closely "heart" as a primal word and gains in this connexion the notion of *real symbol*, he has thereby seized on an important theme of anthropology inasmuch as man's body is the outward form which both reveals and conceals the essence of the person. From this standpoint, the concept of "real symbol" can also become very important also in Christology, ecclesiology and sacramental theology.[71]

Starting out from a modern metaphysic of personality and liberty, Rahner in one of his earliest articles gave new depth to the notion of *concupiscentia*, using the term *Konkupiszenz* to avoid the misunderstandings which sometimes arise from the more usual German translation, *Begierde* ("desire", "lust").[72] "Concupiscence" is the historical, constantly varying diastasis imposed on man's freedom and never completely brought under control in this world of sinners: it exists between "nature" as the material placed at the disposal of liberty and the realization of the person possessed of freedom, who never completely succeeds in integrating his whole "nature" in good or evil in a completely free decision.

He has produced a short book, for the "Quaestiones Disputatae" series, on the *theology of death* from the standpoint of Christian anthropology.[73] Here Rahner is chiefly concerned to get rid of the idea of death as a mere biological exit. Death corresponds to man's unity in that it is a primal occurrence involving the whole man; it is the absolute deed of man accomplished in absolute suffering, the unity of which stretches throughout the whole life in which dying takes place, and thereby is withdrawn from man himself. Through this existential-ontological interpretation of death, as actively taking up a stand in regard to man's existence—in so far as this is something that comes upon him—Rahner is able to conceive death as the extreme act of despair, as *mortal* sin absolutely speaking, or alternatively as the peak of existence in faith, as dying with Christ. But he tries also in this connexion to expose the defects of the traditional description of death as separation of body and soul. The concept, "separation", is obscure and difficult to reconcile with the Catholic teaching that man's spiritual principle of life (called "soul") is *substantially* one with the body. Since the soul precisely through the body is related to the material unity of the world, the "separation" of the soul from the body cannot mean the absolute cessation of this relationship with the world, so that the soul would only exist as extra-mundane. Rahner shows how the human soul in death enters upon a still greater proximity and a more inward relationship to the material source of the world's unity: from this standpoint he is then able to think out afresh the meaning of the part of the "dead" (saints, purgatory) in the historical determination of the world, in so far as their freely undertaken testimony after death pertains to the spiritual reality of the world.

Out of the many works of Karl Rahner in the whole field of *moral theology*, I shall mention only a few titles here. Long before the Holy Office in Rome had taken notice of a false situation-ethics and mysticism of sin, he had decisively opposed these errors of the time.[74] But he had done something much more important: he had just as clearly and at an equally early date underlined the fact that we must see the individual person possessed of freedom and his history, even in the sphere of "what ought to be", not merely as an instance of a universal idea and thus as a pure realization of a universal moral law. However much each individual human being is subject to and remains bound by the universal law (which Christianity proclaims as natural or positive divine law for all), he is and remains equally unique and unrepeatable and therefore has also a function and an obligation which is his and his alone. In this sense, therefore, within a universally binding essential-ethic there is also an existential-ethic.[75]

This existential-ethic cannot, of course, tell the individual human being precisely what is the material content of the requirement imposed by the divine call on him in particular. But it might and indeed ought to offer a formal logic with the aid of which any individual as such can discover God's will for himself. This is a task which has simply not been noticed by theologians (with the exception of one or two great minds, such as Ignatius of Loyola or Cardinal Newman). For the theory is still widespread that the individual can adequately understand his duty by applying the universal moral principles to the concrete, empirically worked out "case". We may simply note in passing that Rahner's conception of morality is also very biblical. For in our Lord's words about the judgment there is nothing about what sins have been "committed", but he does speak of omissions —disregard for the duty of each as an individual. Rahner has examined the theme in Ignatius of Loyola, but has indicated also the practical consequences for the Church's life: that is, with reference to the "charismatic" element of the individual in the Church which those who hold office in the Church have to respect.[76]

Finally, a word about Rahner's *eschatology*. He has tried to set out dogmatic principles for the interpretation of eschatological statements.[77] Protology—that is, the doctrine of the beginning of the world and of man— speaks of historical events, but it is not an eye-witness account of what happened once, but an "aetiological" statement about the beginning as the necessary reason of that reality which is experienced as our own situation of salvation or damnation. This protology becomes ever richer and brighter as redemptive history advances further. Rahner draws from this his conclusion for eschatology, that is, the theology of the Last Things. Christian eschatology is likewise not an account in anticipation of the phenomena of future events. It is rather the projection of Christian cosmology, anthropology and Christology, which make up and interpret our redemptive-

historical present, into man's state of fulfilment. From
this standpoint, Rahner goes on to develop a criterion
(even though it can never be completely adequate) for
distinguishing what is the true, objective meaning in
eschatological statements, and what is merely an imagina-
tive presentation. This clearly means that those who
preach and teach in the Church must speak about these
things more circumspectly and cautiously and maintain
better God's sovereignty over the destiny of the world
and of mankind. Our Lord's words about heaven and
hell were not uttered to satisfy human curiosity, but were
a solemn reminder of the real possibilities with which
the present moment is endowed for man.

In this very imperfect survey, I have tried to show that
Karl Rahner's theology does not consist—as some have
maintained—solely of unanswered questions. It really is
not his life's plan to create unrest for the sake of unrest.
Perhaps it has become clear in the themes collected here
that, in theology at any rate, we cannot spare ourselves
the effort of thinking. An intensive study of the work of
Karl Rahner reveals more answers than questions, particularly in ecumenical discussion and in contemporary
society, shaped as this is by the contemporary world-
picture. The time for systematizing these suggestions is
not yet—nor can we even elucidate them in alphabetical
order. At the end of the Flemish edition of this book,
I wrote: "The work of Karl Rahner will have a deter-
mining influence on Catholic theology even in the twenty-
first century." Today there is no reason to revise or even
modify this optimistic outlook.

Notes and Bibliography

The notes that begin on this page serve also as a form of bibliography of those works by Karl Rahner which have been translated into English as well as of some that have not been translated. Readers looking for a complete bibliography are referred to the Verzeichnis sämtlicher Schriften 1924-1964, *a complete index of all Karl Rahner's books, published in pamphlet form by Verlag Herder, Freiburg im Breisgau, Germany.*

A separate, alphabetical list of all books by Karl Rahner available in English will be found on page 96.

I

1. "Anthropologie" in *Lexikon für Theologie und Kirche*, I (Freiburg i. Br., 1957), coll. 624-5.

2. *Schriften zur Theologie*, III (Einsiedeln, ²1957), pp. 39 f.

3. *Schriften zur Theologie*, I (Einsiedeln, 1954), pp. 15-16. English translation by Cornelius Ernst, O.P., *Theological Investigations*, I (London: Darton, Longman & Todd, and Baltimore: Helicon, 1961), p. 7.

4. *Sendung und Gnade* (Innsbruck, ³1961), p. 34. English translation by Cecily Hastings, *Mission and Grace*, I (London and New York: Sheed & Ward, 1963), p. 35.

5. An excellent account of the nature and outlook of the youth movement of that time is provided by Oskar Köhler under the title of "Jugendbewegung" in *Lexikon für Theologie und Kirche*, V (Freiburg i. Br., 1960), coll. 1181-2.

6. Luciana Frassati, *Das Leben Pier Giorgio Frassatis*, with an Introduction by Karl Rahner (Freiburg i. Br., 1961), pp. 9-10, 12.

7. We owe the following dates of events in Rahner's life to Dr Robert Scherer (Director of Verlag Herder, Freiburg i. Br.) who was closely associated with him throughout these years.

8. *Zur Erde entschlossen* (Frankfurt, 1948); *Der mächtige Gott* (Frankfurt, 1948); *Kämpfer, Beter, Zeuge* (Berlin, 1955).

9. *Geist in Welt* (Munich, ²1957), p. 407. (An English translation is in preparation with Sheed & Ward, London.)

10. *Ibid.*, pp. 13-14.

11. Rahner makes considerable use of the word *Ursprung* ("source", "origin", but perhaps more literally "primal spring"—*Trans.*), on which Honecker commented, "What then is springing (*was springt denn da*)?"

12. *Geist in Welt*, p. 14.

13. Josef de Vries, *Scholastik*, 15 (1940), pp. 404-9.

14. A retreat, based on the *Exercises*, which he gave in the German college in Rome in 1956, was duplicated—as were the scripts of his lectures—and appeared in a third edition with 208 pages at Innsbruck in 1959.

15. An English translation is in preparation with Sheed & Ward, London and New York.

16. *Hörer des Wortes*, p. 203.

17. *Ibid.*, p. 204.

18. *Ibid.*, p. 209.

19. On the life-work of Hugo Rahner, see H. Vorgrimler, *Den Vätern und dem Vater: Der Theologe und Historiker Hugo Rahner* (Bodenseebuch, 1963), under the patronage of Hermann Hesse and others (Kreuzlingen, 1963), pp. 20-30.

20. "A Scheme for a Treatise of Dogmatic Theology" in *Theological Investigations*, I (London: Darton, Longman & Todd, and Baltimore: Helicon, 1961), pp. 19-37.

21. Karl Rudolf, *Aufbau im Widerstand* (Salzburg, 1947), pp. 33, 39, 53, 55, 56, 57, 119.

22. "Exegese und Dogmatik" in *Schriften zur Theologie*, V (Einsiedeln, 1962), pp. 82-111. An English translation of this article appears under the title "Exegesis and Dogmatic Theology" in *Dogmatic versus Biblical Theology*, a collection of important essays edited by Herbert Vorgrimler (London: Burns & Oates, Baltimore: Helicon, and Montreal: Palm Publishers, 1965), pp. 31-66.

23. *Sendung und Gnade*, pp. 345, 352-354. English translation by Cecily Hastings and Richard Strachan, *Mission and Grace*, II (London and New York: Sheed & Ward, 1964), pp. 155-6, 166-8.

24. *Das Problem des Hominisation* (together with P. Overhage), ²1963; "Um des Erscheinungsbild des ersten Menschen" in P. Overhage, *Die Frage nach dem Erscheinungsbild des Menschen* (Freiburg i. Br., 1959), pp. 11-30.

25. Cf. "Das Christentum und die nichtchristlichen Religionen" in *Schriften zur Theologie*, V (Einsiedeln, 1962), pp. 136-158.

26. Latest edition, thoroughly revised by Adolf Schönmetzer, S.J. (Barcelona-Freiburg-Rome-New York, 1965).

27. Two volumes have appeared in English: Burkhard Neunheuser, O.S.B., *Baptism and Confirmation* (London: Herder–

Burns & Oates, Montreal: Palm Publishers, and New York: Herder & Herder, 1965); Bernhard Poschmann, *Penance and the Anointing of the Sick* (London: Herder–Burns & Oates, Montreal: Palm Publishers, and New York: Herder & Herder, 1965).

28. Two supplementary volumes, wholly devoted to the proceedings and the conclusions of Vatican II, will appear as soon as possible.

29. *Über die Schriftinspiration* (Freiburg i. Br., ³1962), p. 9. This general introduction does not appear in the English edition: *Inspiration in the Bible* (London: Herder–Burns & Oates, Montreal: Palm Publishers, and New York: Herder & Herder, ³1965). This essay also appears, in a revised translation, in the volume *Studies in Modern Theology* (London: Herder–Burns & Oates, Montreal: Palm Publishers, and New York: Herder & Herder, 1964).

30. Two of these have appeared in English under the title of *Theological Investigations*. The first, translated by Cornelius Ernst, O.P. (London: Darton, Longman & Todd, and Baltimore: Helicon, 1961); the second translated by Karl-H. Kruger (London: Darton, Longman & Todd, and Baltimore: Helicon, 1963).

31. In English in two volumes, translated by Cecily Hastings: (London and New York: Sheed & Ward; vol. I, 1963; vol. II, 1964); vol. III is in preparation. In America these volumes are published under the title *The Christian Commitment*.

32. London: Burns & Oates, Montreal: Palm Publishers, and Baltimore: Helicon, 1965.

33. Translated by Richard Strachan and edited by Cornelius Ernst, O.P. (London: Herder–Burns & Oates, Montreal: Palm Publishers, and New York: Herder & Herder, 1965).

34. An English translation is in the course of preparation with Herder–Burns & Oates (London), Palm Publishers (Montreal), and Herder & Herder (New York).

35. An English translation is in preparation with Burns & Oates.

36. *Gott in Welt* (Freiburg i. Br., 1964).

II

37. Cf. Gottlieb Söhngen, "Neuscholastik", in *Lexikon für Theologie und Kirche*, VII (Freiburg i. Br., 1962), coll. 923-6.

38. Cf. *Schriften zur Theologie*, I, p. 328; English translation: *Theological Investigations*, I (London and Baltimore, 1961), pp. 311 f.

39. "Über den Begriff des Geheimnisses in der katholischen Theologie" in *Schriften zur Theologie*, IV, ²1962, pp. 51-99.

40. "Zur scholastischen Begrifflichkeit der ungeschaffenen

Gnade" in *Schriften zur Theologie*, I, pp. 347-75; "Probleme der Christologie von heute", *ibid.*, pp. 169-222; "Natur und Gnade" in *Fragen der Theologie heute*, ed. J. Feiner, J. Trütsch, F. Böckle (Einsiedeln, ³1960), pp. 209-30; "Zur Theologie der Menschwerdung" in *Schriften zur Theologie*, IV, pp. 137-55. The first three of these essays are translated: "Some Implications of the Scholastic Concept of Uncreated Grace" in *Theological Investigations*, I, pp. 319-46; "Current Problems in Christology", *ibid.*, pp. 149-200; *Nature and Grace* (translated by Dinah Wharton), London, 1963, pp. 3-44.

41. "Theos im Neuen Testament" in *Schriften zur Theologie*, I, pp. 91-167 (English translation: "Theos in the New Testament" in *Theological Investigations*, I, pp. 79-148); "Bemerkungen zum dogmatischen Traktat 'De Trinitate'" in *Schriften zur Theologie*, IV, pp. 103-33.

42. "Probleme der Christologie von heute" in *Schriften zur Theologie*, I, pp. 169-222; "Auferstehung des Fleisches" in *Schriften zur Theologie*, II, pp. 211-25; "Die ewige Bedeutung der Menschheit Jesu für unser Gottesverhältnis" in *Schriften zur Theologie*, III, pp. 47-60; "Dogmatische Erwägungen über das Wissen und Selbstbewusstsein Christi" in *Schriften zur Theologie*, V, pp. 222-45. The first two of these essays are translated: "Current Problems in Christology" in *Theological Investigations*, I, pp. 149-200; "The Resurrection of the Body" in *Theological Investigations*, II, pp. 203-16.

43. "Hypostatic Union" in *A Concise Theological Dictionary* (London: Herder–Burns & Oates, Montreal: Palm Publishers, and New York: Herder & Herder, 1965).

44. "Zur scholastischen Begrifflicheit der ungeschaffenen Gnade" in *Schriften zur Theologie*, I, pp. 347-75 (in English: "Some Implications of the Scholastic Concept of Uncreated Grace" in *Theological Investigations*, I, pp. 319-46); "Über die Erfahrung der Gnade" in *Schriften zur Theologie*, III, pp. 105-9; "Natur und Gnade" in *Fragen der Theologie heute*, pp. 209-30 (in English: *Nature and Grace* [London and New York: Sheed & Ward, 1964], pp. 3-44.

45. Cf. "Das Christentum und die nichtchristlichen Religionen" in *Schriften zur Theologie*, V, pp. 136-58.

46. *Ibid.*

47. *Das Problem der Hominisation*; "Um das Erscheinungsbild des ersten Menschen" in P. Overhage, *Die Frage nach dem Erscheinungsbild des Menschen*, pp. 11-30; "Erlösungswirklichkeit in der Schöpfungswirklichkeit" in *Sendung und Gnade*, Innsbruck, ³1961, pp. 51-88 (in English: "The Order of Redemption within the Order of Creation" in *Mission and Grace*, I, pp. 59-113).

48. Cf. quotation on pp. 14-15; "Natur und Gnade" in *Fragen der Theologie heute*, pp. 209-30 (in English: *Nature and Grace*, pp. 3-44).

49. *Sendung und Gnade*, Innsbruck, ³1961 (in English: *Mission and Grace* in two volumes (*see* n. 31 above).

50. "Chancen des Christentums heute" in *Das freie Wort in der Kirche* (Einsiedeln, ²1954); "Theologische Deutung der Position des Christens in der modernen Welt" in *Sendung und Gnade*, pp. 13-47 (in English: "A theological Interpretation of the Position of Christians in the modern World" in *Mission and Grace*, I, pp. 3-55); "Würde und Freiheit des Menschen" in *Schriften zur Theologie*, II, pp. 247-77 (in English: "The Dignity and Freedom of Man" in *Theological Investigations*, II, pp. 235-63; "Die Christologie innerhalb einer evolutiven Weltanschauung" in *Schriften zur Theologie*, V, pp. 183-222.

51. *Die vielen Messen und das eine Opfer* (Freiburg, 1951); *Kirche und Sakramente* (Freiburg, ²1961): in English: *The Church and the Sacraments* (London: Herder–Burns & Oates, Montreal: Palm Publishers, and New York: Herder & Herder, ³1964); "Personale und Sakramentale Frommigkeit" in *Schriften zur Theologie*, II, pp. 115-41 (in English: "Personal and Sacramental Piety" in *Theological Investigations*, II, pp. 109-33); "Vergessene Wahrheiten über das Bussakrament", *ibid.*, pp. 143-83 (in English: "Forgotten Truths concerning the Sacrament of Penance" in *Theological Investigations*, II, pp. 135-74); "Bemerkungen zur Theologie des Ablasses", *ibid.*, pp. 185-210 (in English: "Remarks on the Theology of Indulgences" in *Theological Investigations*, II, pp. 175-201); "Die Gegenwart Christi im Sakrament des Herrenmahles" in *Schriften zur Theologie*, IV, pp. 357-97; "Wort und Euchariste", *ibid.*, pp. 313-55.

52. An excellent survey of this period and its intrigues is provided by Oswald von Nell-Breuning in the article, "Integralismus" in *Lexikon für Theologie und Kirche*, V (Freiburg i. Br., 1960), coll. 717 f.

53. "Zur Frage der Dogmenentwicklung" in *Schriften zur Theologie*, I, pp. 49-90 (in English: "The Development of Dogma" in *Theological Investigations*, I, pp. 39-77) and IV, pp. 11-50; "Theologie im Neuen Testament" in *Schriften zur Theologie*, V, pp. 33-53.

54. "Virginitas in Partu" in *Schriften zur Theologie*, IV, pp. 173-205; "Schrift und Tradition" in *Wort und Wahrheit*, 18, 1963, pp. 269-79; also various articles in *Lexikon für Theologie und Kirche*.

55. *Über die Schriftinspiration* (Freiburg, ³1962), in English: *Inspiration in the Bible*; *see* note 29 above.

56. *Episkopat und Primat*, with J. Ratzinger (Freiburg, 1961): in English: *The Episcopate and the Primacy* (London: Herder–Burns & Oates, Montreal: Palm Publishers, and New York: Herder & Herder, 1962, and reprinted under the same imprints in *Studies in Modern Theology*, 1964); "Zur Theologie des Konzils" in *Schriften zur Theologie*, V, pp. 278-302; "Über den Episkopat" in *Stimmen der Zeit* (1963), pp. 161-95 (in English: *Bishops: Their Status and Function*, London: Burns & Oates, and Baltimore: Helicon, 1964).

57. "Die Gliedschaft in der Kirche nach der Lehre der Enzykika Pius' XII. 'Mystici Corporis'" in *Schriften zur Theologie*, II, pp. 7-94. In English: "Membership of the Church according to the Teaching of Pius XII's Encyclical 'Mystici Corporis Christi'" in *Theological Investigations*, II, pp. 1-88.

58. *Kirche der Sünder* (Vienna, 1947); *Das Freie Wort in der Kirche* (Einsiedeln, ²1954); *Das Dynamische in der Kirche* (Freiburg, ³1960), in English: *The Dynamic Element in the Church* (London: Herder–Burns & Oates, Montreal: Palm Publishers, and New York: Herder & Herder, 1964).

59. *Kirche und Sakramente* (Freiburg, ²1961), in English: *The Church and the Sacraments* (London: Herder–Burns & Oates, Montreal: Palm Publishers, and New York: Herder & Herder, ³1964).

60. "Wort und Eucharistie" in *Schriften zur Theologie*, IV, pp. 313-55.

61. *Die vielen Messen und das eine Opfer* (Freiburg, 1951).

62. "Dogmatische Bemerkungen über die Frage der Konzelebration" in *Münchener Theologische Zeitschrift*, 6, 1955, pp. 81-106.

63. "Messopfer und Jugendaszese" in *Sendung und Gnade*, ³1961, pp. 469-89. In English: "The Sacrifice of the Mass and an Ascesis for Youth" in Mission and Grace, I, pp. 203-54.

64. *Diaconia in Christo: Über die Erneuening des Diakonates*, with H. Vorgrimler (Freiburg, 1962); "Über die Erneuerung des Diakonates" in *Sendung und Gnade*, pp. 275-85 (in English: "Deacons" in *Mission and Grace*, II, pp. 53-67), continued in *Schriften zur Theologie*, V, pp. 303-55.

65. "Vergessene Wahrheiten über das Busssakrament" in *Schriften zur Theologie*, II, pp. 143-83. In English: "Forgotten Truths concerning the Sacrament of Penance" in *Theological Investigations*, II, pp. 135-74.

66. "Priesterliche Existenz" in *Schriften zur Theologie*, III, pp. 285-312.

67. *Episkopat und Primat*, with J. Ratzinger (Freiburg, 1961): in English; *see* note 56 above; "Über den Episkopat" in *Stimmen*

der Zeit, 1963, pp. 161-95: in English, *see* note 56 above; "Über Bischofskonferenzen" in *Stimmen der Zeit*, 1963, pp. 267-83.

68. "Zur scholastischen Begrifflichkeit der ungeschaffenen Gnade" in *Schriften zur Theologie*, I, pp. 347-75; in English: "Some Implications of the Scholastic Concept of Uncreated Grace" in *Theological Investigations*, I, pp. 319-47; "Natur und Gnade" in *Fragen der Theologie heute* (Einsiedeln, 1960), pp. 209-30: in English: *Nature and Grace*, pp. 3-44.

69. "Natur und Gnade" in *Fragen der Theologie heute*, pp. 209-30: in English: *Nature and Grace*, pp. 3-44; "Zur Theologie der Menschwerdung" in *Schriften zur Theologie*, IV, pp. 137-55; "Erlösungswirklichkeit in der Schöpfungswirklichkeit" in *Sendung und Gnade*, pp. 51-88: in English: "The Order of Redemption within the Order of Creation" in *Mission and Grace*, I, 1963, pp. 59-113; "Bemerkungen zum dogmatischen Traktat 'De Trinitate' " in *Schriften zur Theologie*, IV, pp. 103-33.

70. "Über die Erfahrung der Gnade" in *Schriften zur Theologie*, III, pp. 105-9.

71. "Zur Theologie der Herz-Jesu-Verehrung" in *Schriften zur Theologie*, III, pp. 379-415; "Zur Theologie des Symbols", *Schriften zur Theologie*, IV, pp. 275-311.

72. "Zum theologischen Begriff der Konkupiszenz" in *Schriften zur Theologie*, I, pp. 377-414. In English: "The theological Concept of Concupiscentia" in *Theological Investigations*, I, pp. 347-82.

73. *Zur Theologie des Todes* (Freiburg, ³1961): in English: *On the Theology of Death*, revised translation (London: Herder–Burns & Oates, Montreal: Palm Publishers, and New York: Herder & Herder, 1964).

74. *Gefahren im heutigen Katholizismus* (Einsiedeln, ³1953): in English: "Dangers in Catholicism Today" in *Nature and Grace*, pp. 47-131.

75. "Über die Frage einer formalen Existentialethik" in *Schriften zur Theologie*, II, pp. 227-46. In English: "On the Question of a Formal Existential Ethics" in *Theological Investigations*, II, pp. 217-434.

76. *Das Dynamische in der Kirche* (Freiburg, ³1960): in English: *The Dynamic Element in the Church* (London: Herder–Burns & Oates, Montreal: Palm Publishers, and New York: Herder & Herder, 1964); *Löscht den Geist nicht aus* (Innsbruck, 1963).

77. "Theologische Prinzipien der Hermeneutik eschatologischer Aussagen" in *Schriften zur Theologie*, IV, pp. 401-28.

Books by Karl Rahner available in English

(Where bibliographical details have already been supplied in the notes beginning on page 89, the appropriate note is indicated within brackets.)

Bishops: Their Status and Function (56).

The Christian Commitment, American title of *Mission and Grace* (31).

A Concise Theological Dictionary (33).

Encounters with Silence (London: Sands, and Westminster, Md.: Newman Press, 1960).

The Eternal Year (32).

Free Speech in the Church (London and New York: Sheed & Ward, 1959).

Happiness through Prayer (Dublin: Clonmore & Reynolds, 1958).

Mary, Mother of the Lord (London: Herder–Nelson, Montreal: Palm Publishers, and New York: Herder & Herder, 1961).

Mission and Grace, 2 vols. (31).

Nature and Grace (44).

Prayers for Meditation, with Hugo Rahner (London: Herder–Nelson, Montreal: Palm Publishers, and New York: Herder & Herder, 1962).

"Quaestiones Disputatae", a series of books of which seven are by Karl Rahner (London: Herder–Burns & Oates, Montreal: Palm Publishers, and New York: Herder & Herder):

The Church and the Sacraments, 1963

The Dynamic Element in the Church, 1964

Hominisation: The Evolutionary Origin of Man as a Theological Problem, 1965.

Inspiration in the Bible, 1961

On Heresy, 1964

On the Theology of Death, 1961

Visions and Prophecies, 1963.

Theological Investigations, 2 vols. (30).